SHAME AND JEALOUSY

Shame and jealousy is one of a series of low-cost books under the title PSYCHOANALYTIC **ideas** which brings together the best of Public Lectures and other writings given by analysts of the British Psycho-Analytic Society on important psychoanalytic subjects.

Other titles in the Psychoanalytic Idea Series:

Dreaming and Thinking
Rosine J. Perelberg (editor)

Spilt Milk: Perinatal Loss and Breakdown
Joan Raphael-Leff (editor)

Unconscious Phantasy
Riccardo Steiner (editor)

Psychosis (Madness)
Paul Williams (editor)

Adolescence
Inge Wise (editor)

The books can be ordered from:
Karnac Books
www.karnacbooks.com
Tel. +(0)20 8969 4454
Fax: +(0)20 8969 5585
E-mail: shop@karnacbooks.com

SHAME AND JEALOUSY

THE HIDDEN TURMOILS

By

Phil Mollon

Series Editors

Inge Wise and *Paul Williams*

KARNAC
LONDON   NEW YORK

First published 2002 by
H. Karnac (Books) Ltd.
6 Pembroke Buildings, London NW10 6RE

Reprinted 2003

Phil Mollon asserts the moral rights to be identified as the author
of this work.

British Library Cataloguing in Publication Data

A C.I.P. for this book is available from the British Library

ISBN: 1 85575 918 7

Edited, designed, and produced by The Studio Publishing Services Ltd,
Exeter EX4 8JN

Printed and bound in Great Britain by Biddles Ltd, *www.biddles.co.uk*

10 9 8 7 6 5 4 3 2

www.karnacbooks.com

To a Bird Called Hope

The bird of hope landed softly on my perch,
With her sweet song she flirted,
And enchanted me,
Then spread her coloured wings,
And I pursued her,
Soaring high,
And low,
We rested in the forest,
Where she dallied with another,
Then the black knight of jealousy,
Riding roughshod in my heart,
Trampled her to death,
And I was ashamed.

Poem by "Pedro"—used with permission

CONTENTS

viii CONTENTS

ACKNOWLEDGEMENTS

I am extremely grateful to Inge Wise for inviting me to write this book, and also for her encouragement over the years in a variety of ways. This is also an opportunity to thank various people whose support helped to sustain me during those times when adverse circumstances made my own psychoanalytic journey extremely arduous; many must remain nameless, but I would particularly like to thank my analyst, Patrick Casement, and supervisors, Eric Rayner and Harold Stewart; the support of my wife, Ros, was also crucial. I would not have been able to write this book without the excellent library services of both the Institute of Psychoanalysis and the Lister Hospital. I would also like to thank Lisa Willis for helpful comments on the manuscript. Appreciation must also be expressed to the many patients who, in their willingness to share their most private areas of mind, have enabled the ideas and perspectives expressed here to emerge; without them there could be no book.

RS - no discourse on the human
affects

- /Foreword /
Include more ± s'con gps oth gp.
∂ shame affects
Also how this may have
contrib. to AG:
discrepancy betw. what I was
experiencing in training + what
was sd. to gps

- {th of sex in gp}
Reason it's lacking —

1) sociological approach
Birkitt
sex the most individual
e.g. sexual fantasy
∂ masturbn —
everything these are fully
social , ∂ hidden

2) anx abt the opening
the sex subj — in gp
what nt. happen:
fear of shame + re-sharing
breaking the facade /
silence ar-d sex-ty

PREFACE

S hame and jealousy are hidden turmoils that pervade human life, exerting their secret terror and control from within. Neither is easily acknowledged. Both are "shame-full". In the gaps and clumsy steps in human intercourse, in the misunderstandings, the misperceptions, and misjudgements, in the blank mocking eyes where empathy should be, in the look of disgust where a smile was anticipated, in the loneliness and disappointment of inarticulate desire that cannot be communicated because the words cannot be found, in the terrible hopeless absence when human connection fails, and in the empty yet rage-filled desolation of abuse—there in these holes and missing bits lies shame. Shame is where we fail. And the most fundamental failure is the failure to connect with other human beings—originally the mother. Jealousy lies in our perception that there is an other (originally the Oedipal other, or a sibling) who might succeed in connecting where we have failed.

The baby seeks its self in the mother's responsive smiling face. Similarly the adult seeks affirmation in the recognition of partner, family, and the community. Except for those who have felt insurmountably secure in the love and validation of the early care-givers, the threat of the blank look of non-recognition is ever-present—or the look that sees not who we wish to be but who the other wishes us to be:

> The "drain hole" look of the Other sucks out who I am for myself, reconstituting it through the perception of one who is not myself. [Kilborne, 1999, p. 42]

When a person seeks help from a psychoanalyst or psychotherapist, the situation is saturated with the potential for shame. The reasons are basically twofold. First, the emotional information to be communicated is inherently of a private, and therefore latently shameful nature. Second, the possibilities of misunderstandings, failures of communication, and inadequacies of empathy are manifold. Astonishingly, this shame-laden quality of the psychoanalytic and psychotherapeutic setting is rarely addressed. Perhaps this becomes less surprising when the "always hidden" nature of shame is appreciated—for shame that is overt and exposed is like a fox forcibly dug out of its lair, when the hounds have exhausted its capacity to flee and hide. Mostly shame lurks unseen.

One of the reasons we avoid speaking of shame may be because it is peculiarly contagious (Lewis, 1971). Hearing of shame evokes shame (even if only subtly and slightly). We do not like it—and so we prefer to speak of something else, such as guilt or envy.

I first became interested in shame when working at the Tavistock Clinic in the early 1980s. By coincidence, I had several patients who presented with particular problems in the area of shame and false self. At the time relatively little had been written about shame from a psychoanalytic and psychological point of view. Thus Nathanson (1987) commented:

> Shame seems to be an emotion little discussed in our clinical work. In the 20 years I have stayed awake at case conferences, attended lectures professional meetings, and symposia, I have never heard a single case in which embarrassment, ridicule, humiliation, mortification, or any other of the shame family of emotions was discussed. ... I began to comprehend that the ubiquity of shame-laden situations was matched by what appeared to be a culture-wide avoidance of pertinent discussion. [Nathanson, 1987b, pp. vii–viii]

Since then, the situation has changed enormously. Psychoanalysts, developmental psychologists, social scientists, and neuroscientists have all made significant contributions to the understanding of shame. A particularly interesting new field, with considerable potential to link with psychoanalysis, is that of evolutionary psychology, which explores how a modern Darwinian perspective (on the selection pressures for the transmission of genes) throws light on aspects of behaviour and emotion that are otherwise obscure (Migone & Liotti, 1998). This illuminates both shame and jealousy in intriguing new ways. In this book I have tried to draw together some of these strands and indicate their relevance to clinical thinking.

The insights of the consulting room are too valuable to be kept for psychoanalysts and related practitioners. Therefore I hope that this exploration of shame and jealousy may be accessible to a more general reader. I have endeavoured to bear this aim in mind as I have written. However, some aspects will inevitably appear puzzling to a reader without any knowledge of psychoanalysis. Therefore I have included an appendix briefly outlining some relevant points about psychoanalytic theory and practice.

A note on clinical illustrations

The book contains numerous clinical illustrations, from both psychoanalysis and psychoanalytic psychotherapy. Some are fictional composites, based on experiences with a number of different patients. Where disguised accounts of work with specific patients are presented, written permission has been obtained. The principles regarding use of disguised clinical material in psychoanalytic publishing discussed by Gabbard (2000) have been followed.

CHAPTER ONE

Shame and jealousy

Panic in the classroom

A homosexual man in psychoanalytic psychotherapy was reflecting upon his residual feelings of anxiety about revealing his sexual orientation. He suddenly recalled an incident at school when he was age twelve. At that time, he had begun to notice a good-looking boy in another class and would often steal a secret glance at him. One day he found himself in the same class as this boy and suddenly believed he overheard him making some reference to his looking. Overwhelmed with shame and panic, and terrified the whole class would discover his secret, he fled from the room.

An anxious manager

A middle manager was required periodically to make business presentations to groups of staff. Mostly he managed this reasonably competently. However, during a period when he was feeling quite depressed he failed to make adequate preparations and also, to his

1

horror, found that he was unable to ad lib and think on his feet in the way he usually had been able to. On one disastrous occasion he found himself completely lost for words, panicking, unable to think, sweating profusely, feeling about to faint—and basically suffering all the features of a panic attack. He felt profoundly humiliated and devastatingly shamed by his own failure and his vision of the surprised and concerned looks on the faces of his audience. Following this, he felt increasingly anxious about any prospect of having to make any kind of public presentation. Eventually he became completely disabled by shame anxiety.

A sexual assault

A young adolescent girl was cornered by a gang of slightly older teenagers. A youth in the group raped her in front of the others. None attempted to help her. Some laughed and jeered and encouraged the rapist. Following this, the girl became increasingly withdrawn, rarely leaving her house. She was haunted, not only by the horror of the assault itself, but also by the image of all the faces looking on at her without concern or empathy and by the thought of the story of her humiliation being spread maliciously around amongst all the youth of the small town. Some months later she had a psychotic breakdown, believing that she had been impregnated by the devil. The accumulating shame had reached intolerable levels. Eventually she made a serious suicide attempt. Shame can be lethal.

Violent responses to shame

A man who had experienced repeated scorn and humiliation from his mother, involving physical, emotional, and sexual abuse, was frequently in danger of falling into states of severely toxic shame. With his girlfriend he would often insist that she reassure him about the quality of his physical, mental, and sexual attributes, becoming enraged if she did not successfully support his fragile self-esteem and sense of masculinity. Sometimes, he would speak scornfully of other people, particularly older women, describing them as "pathetic" and would demand that his girlfriend agree with him. If she hesitated, he would launch into a tirade about how *she* was "pathetic", and on some occasions would terrify her with his violence. It was clear that this shame-ridden man was continually projecting his own self-image as "pathetic" into women representing his abusive mother (i.e. trying to send the shame back where it came from) and demanding his girlfriend's support in this projection. If she failed to comply, then he would attempt to force *her*, through his violence and intimidation to represent and experience the quality of "pathetic". Shame can be very dangerous.

The Hungarian psychoanalyst, Grunberger, gives the following example:

> Some years ago there was an account in Canadian and other newspapers of how a drunkard behaved badly in a pub, and the owner asked him to leave; in other words, he was "treated like dirt". Afterwards he came back armed with a Molotov cocktail and "blew up the joint". There were no survivors. This can be explained as his desire to make his narcissistic injury null and void by causing all those who were witnesses to disappear. [Grunberger, 1989, p. 37]

A vision of shame

A male student visited the flat of his new girlfriend, with whom he was very much in love, clutching a bunch of flowers for his beloved. Finding the door open, he ventured in. Through the open door to the bedroom, he saw her having sex with an old boyfriend. Engrossed in their pleasure, neither of the lovers were aware of his presence as he stood transfixed in horrified fascination. After a few seconds, he quickly but quietly retreated, feeling utterly mortified with shame and embarrassment. Later feelings of humiliation and anger developed. All that night his heart was pounding with such force that he feared his chest would burst. Because of these violent feelings of shame he could not bring himself to contact her. Indeed he wished, in part, that he might never see her again since he could not imagine how he could confront her with his observations without the two of them being consumed with shame and embarrassment. Shame can powerfully inhibit communication of what is most important in a relationship.

Pedro and Natalie

Some years ago I had the interesting opportunity to work with two people, Pedro and Natalie, who sought help as a couple, presenting with particular problems of shame and jealousy. Pedro clearly loved Natalie deeply, enjoying all forms of contact and interaction with her. He delighted in hearing her talk of her experiences, her thoughts, and feelings. In turn he found joy in sharing with her his most vulnerable hopes and dreams. She clearly loved him too. However, for reasons of fears of feeling trapped and suffocated in relationships, derived from her childhood experiences with an invasive and controlling mother, she would be compulsively promiscuous. She felt shame and guilt about this, but was convinced that her sexual adventures were necessary for her psychic survival—representing for her an affirmation of her autonomy and sense of agency and efficacy. In order not to hurt Pedro, she would try to conceal these from him—but they would usually emerge, partly because Pedro was very perceptive and attuned to her, and partly because her feelings of guilt would lead her to betray herself and reveal her deceit.

Pedro described his feelings and reactions at such times of discovery of her infidelities. He would experience a violent visceral response—pain in his stomach, his heart pounding, shivering and sweating—as his body was clearly flooded with adrenalin. He would also experience a sense of shock, accompanied by anxiety, anger, and panic. He would feel confused and disoriented. In addition he would feel shame. His sense of shame would be to do with feeling inadequate as a man, feeling humiliated by the thought of another man having penetrated the woman he loved, perhaps giving her more pleasure than he managed to, feeling weak and in need of reassurance that he was still loved—and, above all, shame to do with having these strong reactions.[1] This constellation of shame, jealousy, and panic would be exacerbated by Natalie's tendency to attempt to ward off Pedro's suspicions of her infidelities by denying and invalidating his intuitions and dismissing them as his jealous *fantasies*. Her well-meaning effort to avoid his encounter with a painful reality would add to the shocking impact of his eventual discoveries of the truth. Pedro would then feel utterly betrayed and tricked. Their previous intimacy would suddenly appear to him quite fraudulent. The love she had appeared to give him would seem devalued, since Pedro now imagined that she would give the same affection to any of her lovers. Natalie would become distraught at his reactions, feeling terribly guilty at his distress. She would endeavour to reassure him of her love in every way she could. Usually, after a week or two of experiencing her devoted affection and care, Pedro would forgive her again and begin once more to enjoy their time with each other—until the next episode of her infidelity. This painful cycle would repeat endlessly.

Another feature of Pedro's reactions would be that when he learned of her unfaithfulness he would have an odd sensation that she had suddenly become a stranger to him. He would feel that somehow he did not know her. It seems to be a fundamental human need to feel special and chosen—and much of the time this was indeed how Pedro felt in relation to Natalie. However, on discovering her extra-relational sexual liaisons, he would each time feel suddenly in the position of the excluded one—barred access to her intimacy that she experienced with an other—and barred from knowledge of it.

At times Natalie's involvements with other men would go further than brief sexual encounters. She would occasionally develop preoccupations with particular men, wanting continuing contact and, for a limited period, feeling she was in love. After a few weeks this would pass and her affections would again return to Pedro. During such times Pedro would sense her preoccupation and would feel intense anguish because he knew her mind was not open to his emotional communications. Although Natalie would not entirely ignore him, he would experience a subtle blankness in her response to him, as if his messages did not quite penetrate her mind but bounced off its surface. He would complain she was like a brick wall. Such remarks would puzzle her. Pedro would himself withdraw when he found Natalie in such a state, feeling a combination of shame and despair. His attempts to communicate with her seemed to him futile.

The painful cycle of interaction would be further driven by Natalie's experience of feeling her inner privacy to be agonizingly violated by Pedro's wishes to know of both her desires and her behaviour in relation to other men. This led Natalie to feel even more strongly that the integrity of her core self required that she be free to pursue other liaisons outside her main relationship with Pedro, which she would otherwise experience as unbearably suffocating. She would become even more withdrawn in response to his inquiries. Whilst Pedro tried his best to understand her need for inner space, privacy, and freedom, he experienced difficulty in containing his jealousy, further fuelled by Natalie's resistance to disclosing her extra-relational fantasies and behaviours. Moreover, he felt shame over his jealousy, no matter how inevitable and understandable this might be. He felt that his possessiveness drove Natalie to her promiscuity. When in the grip of this spiralling negative interaction, Pedro began to feel very inadequate. Natalie, in turn, felt immense shame and guilt that her compulsive behaviour caused Pedro such distress. It was in their despair at this repeating pattern of pain that this couple, who clearly loved each other dearly, sought psychotherapeutic help. Fortunately, their commitment to communication and their increasing empathy with each other's experience and position provided considerable relief and the negative interaction gradually decreased in intensity; Natalie began to experience less of a threat to her core self, and consequently was less driven to secret promiscuity, with the result that Pedro's jealousy and shame were less and less provoked.

Natalie's mother appeared to have been highly invasive and controlling, insisting that her daughter have no secrets from her. She would frequently demand to know Natalie's thoughts and feelings. Natalie's father was ejected by her mother when Natalie was aged five. This added to Natalie's image of her mother as terrifyingly controlling and powerful. Her fundamental "internal working model" of attachment relationships (Bowlby, 1980) was that she could be controlled and suffocated. Whilst she longed for intimacy and reliable love, she also desperately needed to feel free. This was a matter of the protection of her core sense of self and its need for autonomy. Pedro's mother had not been so invasive, but he had experienced her, at times, as alarmingly distant and withdrawn. He recalled how she would often appear deeply preoccupied, such that she would be physically but not emotionally present. During such periods Pedro's attempts to communicate his emotional needs would seem to be ignored or misunderstood by his mother. However, Pedro learned as a child that his mother's responsiveness to him would return after a period of time. The nature of her preoccupation and withdrawal was not clear to Pedro. He wondered whether she had experienced episodes of depression or whether she had had an affair during part of his childhood. Although his father had been present, he had, affectively, not been very available to Pedro, tending to spend his leisure hours at the pub or slumped in front of the television.

Themes of shame and jealousy with "Natalie and Pedro"

Jealousy and shame are intimately entwined in the tragic interaction between Pedro and Natalie. She was defending against the threat of violation of her core self—a catastrophe involving ultimate exposure of her inner privacy and surrender to control by an other. Such violation of the core self can be experienced as a rape of the mind—indeed of the soul—and as damaging, potentially, as a physical rape. The emotional response to violation is shame. Natalie's ensuing promiscuity evoked jealousy in Pedro, also giving rise to his feelings of shame associated with a sense of inadequacy. His spiral of shame gathered its own momentum as he then felt shame about his own reactions of jealousy, anger, and shame (i.e. shame about shame). As Natalie withdrew from him and he experienced her as an emotional "brick wall", he felt his attempts at communication of his feelings were unwelcome—and again his response was shame. An associated experience was his perception of Natalie as a "stranger" when her infidelities became apparent; at such times he felt he did not know how to relate to her—he felt he did not *know* her and felt awkward, as one might with a stranger. During periods of loving intimacy with Natalie, Pedro would experience a joyful sense of being special to her, of being her "chosen one" and he would bask in the warmth of her affection. Then each time one of her infidelities became apparent, Pedro would feel violently ejected from his place of intimacy with her— thrown into a profoundly painful place of exclusion and shame— and would feel that *he* was the stranger, looking on with anguished envy at the union of his beloved with an other. In turn, Natalie would feel shamefully exposed whenever her sexual adventures and affairs came to light. As each struggled with their particular forms of shame, they found the only relief lay in communication, whereby they could again and again re-find their empathy for one another. They found that the cure for shame is empathy.

Some of Natalie's shame was to do with feeling violated. Pedro's was associated with feeling excluded or rejected, and ejected from his place of feeling "special" and "chosen". Both of them experienced shame about certain feelings and behaviours being exposed to the anticipated disapproval of the other. What do these various forms of shame have in common? They are all to do with vulnerability in the expression of emotional need in relation to the other person. In each instance the bond of empathy is breached— the experience is of falling out of attunement and into a place of affective loneliness. The experience of subject relating to subject is lost, perhaps abruptly and with emotional violence. In its place is the sense of being dismissed as a subject and of becoming an object to the other.

The positive function of the lie

As Natalie revealed more about her way of being and relating, it became apparent that in many ways she had tended to structure her life around lies and deception. Despite her clear wish to be truthful, and her professed valuing of honesty, she was in certain respects a compulsive liar. Although lies and lying have, in general, highly negative connotations, being seen as forms of manic manipulation and exploitation of others, it was possible to discern a more benign meaning in Natalie's case. For her, the capacity to lie was an expression of her autonomy and privacy. Having experienced her mother as so invasive and controlling, the discovery that it was possible to lie and conceal truth from her mother was of vital significance. It was an affirmation of her separateness from her mother and an indication of her own sense of agency. If she could lie successfully, it must mean that she had a private core self—wherein she could discover her own hidden desire, fantasy, and direction. In her lies, Natalie would feel triumphant, celebrating her secret freedom. Conversely, when her lies were exposed she would feel shame, her inner privacy violated; she would feel deflated and depressed. However, Natalie's lies also caused her great anxiety in her adult relationships. Her wish to be able to have a relationship of

honest intimacy with Pedro conflicted fundamen
that her pervasive pattern was to structure he
concealment. Each person in her life would know
but none would know all of her—although each v
she was presenting a truthful account of herself. Sl
the leakage between the compartmentalized ar_ _ _ _ _ _ _ _ _ _ _
although she also longed to be released from her self-imposed web
of lies. The more that Natalie sought honesty in her relationship
with Pedro the greater her anxiety and sense of crisis. Part of the
therapeutic work was for Natalie to discover that honesty did not
have to mean violation of her core self—and to realize that whilst
she certainly had the capacity to lie and conceal successfully, she
could *choose* to be truthful.

Whilst for Natalie the lie had a positive function, of affirming
privacy and autonomy, its negative aspect is often more apparent.
Through the lie, the child discovers his or her separateness from the
mother. Whilst facilitating the child's process of separation–
individuation, this also evokes a sense of being cut off from
mother's love, according to the formula, "if mother finds out about
my lie she will not love me". The proliferation of the lie means a
continual anxiety of being "found out". Moreover, the compulsive
liar also fails to be truthful to him/herself—and ultimately the
authentic expression of the core self is fundamentally compromised.
The lie is, paradoxically, a failed attempt at preservation of truth—
the truth of the core self.

It begins with a smile

Wouldn't it be awful if the child looked into the mirror and saw
nothing! [a patient quoted by Winnicott, 1967, p. 136]

In the beginning, mother and baby are normally exquisitely attuned
to one another, engaging in highly synchronized "conversations" of
voice and facial expression. Analysis of videorecorded material
shows that the speed of communicative mirroring of facial
expression is extremely fast—responsiveness at fractions of a
second—indicating that mother and baby are processing each
other's emotional messages far faster than conscious awareness

[handwritten annotation: ...and of ch. deals ...ly with mirroring o shame if not ...urest]

makes possible (Hietanen *et al.*, 1998; Schore, 2000). However, if the mother deliberately presents a blank expression, her baby becomes distressed and withdraws in a manner that gives every impression of being a precursor of shame (Broucek, 1982).

If the baby smiles and the mother smiles back, the baby feels recognized and responded to. The baby finds itself in the warmth of the mother's smile.[2] Her smile means that he or she has the capacity to evoke a response—to evoke her love. This is the beginning of the baby's sense of efficacy, which I suggest is based upon the capacity to evoke an emotional response in the other (Broucek, 1979; Mollon, 1993). If there is no response—a blank face—or a response that contains no comprehension of the baby's state, then he or she feels fundamentally impotent, ineffectual, having no emotional significance.

Winnicott described the mirror role of the mother in terms of her enabling the baby to see herself. When the mother looks into the baby's eyes, what the mother "looks like is related to what she sees there", and because the mother from the beginning holds her baby in mind as a whole person, the baby who looks into the mother's face "sees himself or herself" (Winnicott, 1967, p. 131). When this necessary mirroring communication does not take place, however, such babies "look and they do not see themselves" (p. 131). Whilst there are various aspects of the structure and experience of self (Mollon, 1993), one crucial component concerns the sense of who one is for the other (originally the mother). If the early experience is of not existing as a real person for the mother, then a feeling of unreality will be inherent in the sense of self.

It is the same in adult life too. A person smiles at us—a smile of genuine affection and friendship—and we feel warmed by the energy of their love. We feel recognized and valued. If we fail to elicit a smile when we anticipate or hope for one, then we feel rejected, diminished, and aware of a drop in our emotional temperature. Our self-esteem momentarily falls. Whereas in response to the smile, we feel confident about moving forward, expecting acceptance, with the absence of the smile, or the blank face, we feel uncertain, hesitant—and in the grip of a background state of shame. Whilst we might try to ignore such subtleties of experience as we press on with the day to day tasks of life, nevertheless they are there making their mark on our emotions and behaviour. In the case of Pedro and Natalie, Pedro would feel painfully uncertain and hesitant when Natalie was in one of her withdrawn and unresponsive states of mind.

For the baby who experiences the mother's face as responsive not to the baby, but as reflecting only her own moods and preoccupations, the consequences can be serious. Winnicott described how some babies will learn to, "study the maternal visage in an attempt to predict the mother's mood, just exactly as we all study the weather", and will draw emotional conclusions from the observations:

> The baby quickly learns to make a forecast: "Just now it is safe to forget the mother's mood and to be spontaneous, but any minute the mother's face will become fixed or her mood will dominate and my own personal needs must then be withdrawn otherwise my central self will suffer insult." [Winnicott, 1967]

In optimum early life, the small child will experience many episodes of pleasurable attunement with his or her mother. These have a very important function in regulating the child's self-esteem and reducing the propensity for shame (Schore, 1991). Inevitably, however, reality presents elements that disrupt the child's sense of oneness with the mother. Included amongst these disruptive elements are the child's own wishes to separate from the mother and assert autonomy—themes which Erikson (1950) linked with the stage of development concerned with establishing control over the anal sphincter and the discovery of a choice over whether to comply with mother's will or not during "potty training". Erikson described this phase as characterized by a tension between autonomy, on the one hand, and shame and doubt, on the other hand.

Seidler (2000) notes that situations of shame are always "envisaged", i.e. involve exposure to the gaze of others. Since our sense of self is formed in the context of relationship with others, involving the capacity to envisage oneself in the eyes of the other (G. H. Mead, 1934), it follows that shame is inherent in the formation of the self. According to Winnicott's formula, the baby's experience of self rests upon the principle "I am seen, therefore I exist." However, the gaze of the other (primarily mother) will not always be approving and loving; as well as at times not seeing the child's subjectivity, her look may be disapproving and hostile, *hypothesize mini is what happens — in sexual fantasy*

NB?

generating rather global feelings in the small child of being "bad". The problem is that the gaze of the other, even if dysphoria-inducing, is necessary for the development of the self. Seidler (2000) comments as follows:

> If the gaze of the other is experienced not only as judgemental but as censorious, and thus as ascribing to the self bad characteristics ... the result will be an identification of the self as "bad". The urge to eliminate an other experienced as a disruptive force will then recursively weaken the self or the subject because it needs the gaze of the other as a condition of its existence. [p. 179]

The stranger, the father, and the primal scene

From the age of about eight months, the child becomes aware of "strangers" and displays withdrawal and gaze aversion (just like the "shy" adult). For the child who wishes to retain all the good elements of experience in relation to the mother and project the bad elements into the outer world, the stranger will be felt to embody all that is threatening to the oneness with mother. When it is the mother's smiling face that is sought, the unrecognized and alien face of the stranger will represent the bogey man who will destroy the child's paradise with the mother. The small child sees that the mother has some kind of relationship with the stranger, from which the child is excluded. At the same time, under the pressure of the drive for separation–individuation, the stranger may take on a fascination because he also represents the possibility of separation from the mother.

Perhaps the original stranger is the father. Certainly, as Seidler (2000) argues, the child's perception of the mother's relationship with the stranger may be a precursor of the encounter with the primal scene of the parental relationship and intercourse, from which the child is excluded. Seidler describes the child's changing desires as the perception or fantasy of the primal scene is apprehended:

> Whereas previously, unconscious union with the mother was "happiness", that happiness is now located in the "primal scene", in accordance with the logic directing that "happiness is where I am not allowed to be". [Seidler, 2000, p. 191]

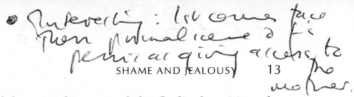

With the advent of the primal scene and the Oedipal position, the child is placed in the position of the outsider:

> a stranger debarred from the union of two others permitted access to a forbidden sphere. [Seidler, 2000, p. 191]

At an earlier stage the child's concern lies with the face, the attunement of the mother's face and the unfamiliar face of the stranger, but in the Oedipal position and the fantasy of the parental primal scene the father's penis represents the "ticket of admission" to fulfilment of the wish for union with the mother. Neither gender of child will feel adequately equipped anatomically nor psychologically to engage in sexual union with the mother—a narcissistic trauma emphasized particularly by Grunberger (1989). Whilst the small child can competently engage in visual facial communication of love and desire for union or affectionate contact with the mother, the impact of the primal scene and the Oedipal situation confronts him or her with a domain of intimacy that is foreign and bewildering—and from which he or she is inherently excluded. The pain of this narcissistic injury can be profound and is universally repressed—its impact revealed only through psychoanalysis. As Grunberger notes, it is "infinitely more difficult to grasp [than oedipal rivalry] and has a tendency to resist analysis until the end" (Grunberger, 1989, p. 37). This deep injury to self-esteem and the sense of adequacy is re-evoked in later situations of adult life when a lover turns to another—as experienced by Pedro in relation to Natalie's infidelities. A novel insight by Grunberger is that the classically conceived Oedipal situation of rivalry can function as a defence against the child's deeper narcissistic injury of sexual inadequacy:

> ... I have insisted many times on the role of the Oedipal interdiction as a defence against the narcissistic injury expressed in the thought: "I am not impotent; it is the other person who is blocking the road (but when I am like him, I shall be able to marry Mother without exposing myself to the repetition of the same narcissistic injury, since I shall be an adult myself)." ... things introduce themselves differently to the girl and to the boy, if only because the narcissistic injury of the girl is less dramatic and more profound: on the one hand she can hide her inadequacy from herself or transform it into a fear of penetration; on the other hand, her injury in the form of penis

envy may stretch across her psychosexual life in general. [Grunberger, 1989, p. 37]

Seidler notes, that from this perspective, the fear of castration, originally emphasized by Freud, can be understood as anxiety about loss of the organ that allows the participants of the primal scene to engage in a union. Sexuality, both that of the child and that of the parents is a highly disturbing and disruptive factor destroying the child's dream of endless union with the mother. Seidler summarizes the situation as follows:

> ... the oedipal situation stage of development proper is characterised by the fact that the previously intended aim of union with a person is ousted by the awareness of that person's connections with what was hitherto a stranger; this finds its symbolisation in the imago of the primal scene. The effect of this is that the child takes the place of the stranger hitherto thwarting its efforts at establishing union, and thus excluding it from the state of felicity that has obviously been realised between the other two. The child thus relates to the primal scene as a stranger. The perception of its own sexual need finds its correspondence in body shame, which through the compounding with the recognition of its own relative sexual inadequacy takes on a quality approximating that of an "experience of inferiority". [Seidler, 2000, pp. 198–199]

The child's encounter with sexuality, his or her own and that of the parents, is inherently disturbing. *Sexuality is traumatic*, as Bollas (2000) argues in his discussion of hysteria:

> ... sexuality destroys the innocence of a self and mother, transforming the prelapsarian utopia of "baba" and "mama" into the world of self and sex object, contaminating the simplicity of dependence with desire ... Sexuality-in-itself, intensified ... by the child's auto-erotic stimulations, is the agency of trauma, all by its fearsome self. [Bollas, 2000, p. 14]

Bollas argues that whilst we cannot remember directly the "sexual epiphany" at age three, it is relatively easy to remember analogous disturbance some years later. Although sexual states of mind do occur at ages seven, eight, or nine, many people tend to remember these years as relatively idyllic. Bollas describes the disturbance as puberty arrives:

Then sometime around 10—earlier for some, later for others—bodies start changing again. With the changing shape of the body, which—however anticipated and partly welcomed—is to some extent disconcerting, comes another increase in sexual excitation. The adolescent feels assaulted by sexual ideas. Sitting in a classroom with childhood friends of old, suddenly a 13-year-old is deeply excited by another student, and finds it very hard to think about the lesson. That other student need not be in the classroom. The instinct is provocation enough for the adolescent to feel its disruptiveness whilst furtively daydreaming his or her sex objects. [Bollas, 2000, p. 17]

We might add to Bollas' account here, the considerable alarm and shame that pubertal boys can experience when erections and nocturnal emissions become frequent and unpredictable. The penis can seem literally to have taken on a life of its own, asserting its presence all too visibly even when the boy is not consciously entertaining sexual thoughts.

A woman with anorexia nervosa described the impact on her of the precocious arrival of puberty. She felt utterly confused and filled with shame at the changes in her body. None of her peers had started menstruating and developing breasts as she had. She felt overwhelmingly self-conscious and out of control. A deep sense of rage accompanied her feeling that she had been prematurely deprived of childhood. Later she completely repudiated her role as an adult sexual woman, welcoming with considerable relief the cessation of her periods and loss of her curvy body as she discovered the "time-reversing" effects of starvation. She took to reading books and magazines written for girls in early adolescence, finding comfort and reassurance in their explanations and preparations for teenage years.

Shame and the false self

Shame and false self developments are intimately entwined.

False self and failure of the Oedipal position

Many psychological problems arise from a failure to negotiate the Oedipal position as a result of the mother's gratification of the child's fantasy of successfully excluding the rival father (Mollon, 1993). Although the child may wish to claim triumphant possession of the mother, gratification of this desire can be disastrous developmentally—resulting not only in fears of being revealed as an impostor, a child pretending to be grown-up, but also in a failure to establish secure boundaries from the mother, and consequently a continual dread of re-engulfment and loss of self-demarcation. The Oedipal "Law of the Father" (Lacan, 1977), that prohibits both mother and child from consuming each other, has been eluded. This can form part of the basis of a "false self" development since the child will be forever trying to be what the mother wants.

Seidler puts this as follows:

> Here the subject is concerned to please the vis-à-vis with a view to gratifying the regressive wish for total attunement. It will thus behave in such a way as to correspond to what it takes to be the other's preferences. The clinical situation in the treatment of such patients confirms this supposition. What is most difficult is the separation from the wish to attune and to be accepted without reserve. Such a phase of treatment is normally characterised not only by the experience of loneliness but also by despair and the irruption of the feeling of being at fault that has been so carefully fended off hitherto. Therapist and patient will come into contact with shame at a primary level, i.e. when the shame-specific wish to be recognised becomes susceptible of experience. In such cases, the incipient capacity for feeling shame is equivalent to the advent of a new dawn. Perception by the other (or in an internalised form as the subject's own judgemental function) has then reached a tolerable stage and no longer demands (subjective) self-abandonment. [Seidler, 2000, p. 180]

What Seidler seems to be pointing to here is the way in which the emergence of a more authentic self, from a position of false self concealment, is associated with shame. It is precisely the true elements of self that are felt to elicit disapproval or non-recognition. Without the Oedipal ejection from the dyadic entanglement with the mother, and the projection into the triadic space, the child may be unable to proceed along the line of separation–individuation. He or she continues to try to be the child the mother wants—the mother's phallus—rather than following his or her own developmental initiatives. This can be a fulfilment of the mother's grandiosity, where her child's function is to cast her in a favourable light. What may appear as an air of superiority in some patients with significant degrees of false self development may actually be this kind of expression of the mother's narcissism. In such a person, their own desires and initiatives, and natural exhibitionism, may be associated with much shame and anxiety, and as a result may be repressed—emerging only against great resistance in the process of analysis or psychotherapy. These difficulties are described in detail in Kohut (1971).

The shame associated with emergence from a false self position is to do with the expectation that the more authentic feelings and aspirations (the "true self") will not be recognized, understood or accepted. It is akin to emerging from behind a mask, or taking off a costume, or exposing oneself as having been a fraud or impostor. The fear is that this will be an *embarrassing* shock to the other. In general, situations of embarrassment always involve some kind of disruption of the expectations one person has of another. It follows, then, that for the person who has developed an extensive false self the more authentic aspects of self will be felt as an embarrassment. There will tend to be a continual monitoring of the presentation of "self", so as to fit in with the expectations and desires of the other. This is the basis of embarrassed self-consciousness. Shame and embarrassment arise in the jarring cracks between the expectation of the other and the actual feelings and behaviour of the self.

The person with an extensive false self development has become trapped in an image—the image of the child the mother wanted him or her to be. Instead of having felt recognized and accepted as himself, his own potential being nurtured, the child has become inhabited by the mother's fantasy. Whilst to some extent all human identities are false, insofar as we have to construct a "self" on the basis of the roles and images available in the pre-existing culture into which we are born, this process becomes more tilted in the direction of pathology when the mother's narcissism takes precedence over her concern to recognize and nurture her particular child. The more authentic self then becomes a potential embarrassment and a source of anxiety, along the lines of, "What if my mother/the world in general discovers that I am not what they assume I am—I will be greeted with horrified shock and rejection—this possibility is so terrible that I must make absolutely sure that my real self does not emerge—I must conceal it from myself".

Short trousers

A twelve-year-old boy in Britain in the 1960s, when short trousers were the norm for younger schoolboys, became increasingly embarrassed because he was the only one left in his class who had not graduated to long trousers. His mother expressed reluctance to buy him long trousers on the grounds that she did not like to see children looking too grown-up. The message from this, and other aspects of his mother's behaviour, was that she wanted her son to remain a child, without regard for his own experience, desire, and developmental need. About four-years later, the young man had managed to acquire long trousers, but he became extremely worried and embarrassed because he was increasingly needing to shave but did not have a razor or other equipment. He did not know how to bring this to his parents' attention, fearing again that his developing adult body would be a shocking disruption of his mother's image of him as a child. On the other hand he was afraid that there would come a point when the whiskers on his face would suddenly evoke an expression of horrified surprise from his mother. He did not feel he could confide in his father, who was a rather passive and distant figure, frequently the butt of his mother's criticism and scorn. In such a situation, pervaded by potential embarrassment, the embarrassment that is feared is the embarrassment of the other when their expectation is disrupted.

An alarming dream

A man in psychoanalysis was always smartly dressed and clearly concerned with his appearance and impression on others. He presented an image of a polite, intelligent and cultured gentleman. It was apparent that this very much reflected his mother's desires to have such a child. During the early stages of analysis he would tend to speak quietly and without much emotion, always listening carefully to what the analyst had to say. However, during one session he reported with some anxiety a dream in which a classical music concert was interrupted by the intrusion of a violent and scruffy vagabond who belligerently stormed the stage. This presaged an anxious period in the analysis when his more aggressive and less polite aspects began to emerge. As this process developed he experienced much shame and embarrassment.

The entertainer

Another patient, a woman, had been brought up to perform—her mother having taken every opportunity to put her on stage, despite the patient's natural shyness and dislike of excessive attention. She had developed the beginnings of a career as a dancer and singer. In the analysis she tended to present herself in entertaining ways, telling colourful narratives of her life. However, in her career she displayed a pattern of sabotaging her opportunities, initially without insight into her active and motivated role in this. It was apparent that unconsciously she wished to overthrow the role and image that her mother had foisted upon her. Later in the analysis, she began to present herself in a much more subdued way and the lively stories disappeared. Her motivation to pursue her career as a performer began to diminish. She disclosed, with some shame and embarrassment, that she was writing a novel, but was extremely anxious about the potential reactions of others if she were to show them the content. The patient's overtly "exhibitionistic" performing self was a "false self", based on her mother's desire. Behind this was a repressed "true self", expressed in the private writing—and the tentative emergence of this was associated with much shame and anxiety.

Shame emerges at moments of our deepest psychological vulnerability. Exposure to the risk of shame is inherent in one person's offer of intimacy with an other—and is a measure of the value placed upon that other. Thus the adolescent boy must balance his fear of shame, and the risk of humiliation and rejection, against the strength of his desire when he considers approaching a girl, stuttering and blushing, as he awkwardly asks her out. This is true also of the child who is willing to communicate his or her feelings and needs to the mother or father. Such willingness is not to be taken for granted. Repeated rejection, scorn or gross empathic failure, may lead to an entrenched reluctance to communicate emotional need and a persisting avoidance of intimacy in later life. Too much shame results in an unconscious decision not to risk further exposure. The "true self" goes into hiding.

Summary and conclusion

Shame and the fear of shame are amongst the most powerful of human aversive experiences, precipitating panic, rage, and the wish to disappear—and, in extreme cases, homicide, suicide, and even psychosis. The integrity and preservation of the core self is crucial to shame. Shame arises both from violation of the self, *and* from exposure of the self when this is not met with the expected or hoped for empathy. In a context of empathy, the self and its needs can safely be exposed and expressed—but without empathy the self feels threatened. The presence of shame signals a lack of empathy— either an actual lack, or a fear of such a lack. Similarly, the cure for states of shame and humiliation is empathy—but in its absence, shame expands unchecked, becoming increasingly toxic. When in the grip of shame, the person has no empathy with him/herself— and, without the soothing words or touch of an other—hatred of the self may grow without limit.

By analogy, we might picture the core self as like a flower that can be tightly furled (withdrawn and protected), but under the impact of the warm sunlight (empathy) will unfold, radiating its colour to other living forms and inviting intercourse and fertiliza- tion. If the emotional weather is cold, unexpected or inappropriate in some way (the risk of shame), then the flower may become again enclosed upon itself.

As Seidler comments:

> Shame manifests itself when a subject in quest of attunement encounters something–someone "strange", causing it to recoil back onto itself. [Seidler, 2000, p. 320]

The young child's wishes for attunement with the mother, the enjoyment of basking in mutual love and the mirroring gaze and smile—Kohut's "gleam in the mother's eye"—is disrupted by sexuality (as well as other components of mental life that propel the child towards separation–individuation). The child's sexual desire, and his or her recognition of that of the parents, brings a disturbing and "strange" element into the infantile world. The mother is recognized as having a relationship with the father, from which the child is excluded. It is a relationship that the child does not understand, however much he or she may try to conceptualize this in terms of his own desires and phantasies. In this respect it is unlike the rivalry felt with other siblings (Mitchell, 2000). Through entry into the Oedipal position and the encounter with the primal scene, the child is cast into the place of the stranger, the outsider, the one who is excluded from the paradise of union with the mother.

However, the failure to be cast out of the dyad with the mother —a bypassing of the Oedipal position—can have a catastrophic impact on development. The child has not then been liberated by the "Law of the Father" (Lacan, 1977) and remains imprisoned in an image reflecting the mother's desire. Such derailment of the required trajectory into the triadic space may contribute considerably to pathological degrees of false self development. Aspects of self that do not fit the required image will be associated with shame because of the anticipation that these will be met with disapproval, non-recognition, or bewilderment. Only the prospect of understanding and acceptance—perhaps in psychoanalysis or in a loving relationship—can enable these to emerge and the threat of shame be faced.

Notes

1. The field of evolutionary psychology offers perspectives on both promiscuity and jealousy, showing how both may have been selected for their reproductive advantages (e.g. Buss, 2000).

2. Schore (1994, 1998) presents much developmental and neurobiological evidence that the early interactions with the mother directly affect the young child's developing brain, regulating the levels of dopamine and noradrenaline. Part of the function of the visual facial interaction between mother and infant appears to be to stimulate the child's brain and to regulate arousal. Synchronised gaze interactions generate highly pleasurable states in the infant's brain and these facilitate attachment.

CHAPTER TWO

Shame—further reflections

S hame involves a hole—a hole where our connection to others should be. In shame we fall out of the dance, the choreography of the human theatre. And in the deepest depths of shame we fall into a limbo where there are no words but only silence. In this no-place there are no eyes to see us, for the others have averted their gaze—no-one wishes to see the dread that has no name.

Shame and schizophrenia

This is sometimes conveyed most vividly and painfully by people suffering from schizophrenia. One patient, Sally, described how she would observe other people communicating, with words and gestures, each person seemingly perfectly "in step" and harmonized with the other—an astonishingly intricate interlocking of sound and movement, determined by dauntingly complex rules of form and content, whereby each person apparently conveys meaning to the other. As a child, Sally had always experienced difficulty in "joining in" with others, despite her intense desire to do so. She had never been able to understand how and why people behaved towards each other in the way that they did, and why one kind of behaviour or conversation took place in one situation, but not in another. Increasingly Sally's social experiences had been painful and discouraging, involving rejection, teasing and scorn from her peers who had clearly regarded her as odd. She came to feel ever more awkward in the presence of others, never knowing how to behave or what to say. Her feelings of shame and self-consciousness intensified, crippling her social capacities even further. Finding the social world almost entirely without reward and consistently humiliating, Sally withdrew more and more into her secret alternative world of inner fantasy. She began to devise her own private code of communication involving certain gestures and signals. When imposing this on others she was attempting both to deny her own failure to understand the shared social "language" and to make others feel something of the incomprehension and bewilderment that was her recurrent experience. By late adolescence she had become floridly psychotic.

Sally's behaviour was pervaded by indications of shame, self-consciousness, and embarrassment. When she first began attending her psychotherapy sessions, she would conceal herself behind a pot plant in the waiting area. She would avoid eye contact. She would repeatedly apologize if she felt she might have behaved inappropriately in some way. Moreover, she would report excruciating shame at her recognition that some of her behaviour and remarks would indeed be regarded as odd by others. Sometimes she would attempt to counter her shame by making a point of explicitly telling people that she was schizophrenic almost on first meeting them. It was apparent that she was extremely anxious about telling me of her private thoughts, beliefs, and fantasies, for fear that I would laugh at her or react with shock. Her core fantasy, which varied in its degree of prominence, was that she was the "son of God", with a secret message for the world. I describe this as her "core" fantasy because, although she told me it was always present in her mind, it was the one that she referred to most rarely, and when she did so she was clearly extremely anxious and embarrassed. This self-image, of the utmost grandiosity, obviously functioned in part to counter her feelings of inferiority and inadequacy, but was itself associated with intense shame and for this reason was mostly concealed. I think it is probably the case with many core schizophrenic delusions—they are concealed because of shame and are certainly not revealed to the casual and unempathic enquiries of the general psychiatrist. Probably it is only when the patient is in a fairly florid psychotic state that he or she will display core delusions overtly—at such times of acute psychosis, shame appears absent. Afterwards, when the acute phase has subsided, the patient may suffer terrible shame at the memories of his or her behaviour. The same is true of those patients who at times experience manic states of mind.

Whilst there are no doubt many factors converging to produce the clinical state and personality of schizophrenia, an inability to process and respond appropriately to the communicative signals of others seems crucial. Schizophrenic people have difficulty understanding others and in grasping social rules and expectations in the way that most of us are able to do relatively effortlessly. It is a kind of social dyslexia. In this respect there may be links with other conditions involving failures in grasping social meaning and in understanding the minds of others, such as is found in autism and Asperger syndrome (Concoran, 2000; Frith, 1994). The problem may arise from neurobiological abnormalities that result in difficulties in processing emotional and social information, and impairments of the normal filtering, focusing and sorting of perceptual stimuli. Such patients live with the continual threat of engulfment by cognitive and perceptual chaos—the "black hole" of non-meaning (Grotstein, 1977, 1990). Another contributing factor may be confusions and contradictions inherent in the communications of the mother, such that the child who becomes schizophrenic cannot "make sense" of her messages—although I do not wish to suggest that this is a primary or essential cause of schizophrenia, which almost certainly has some basis in neurobiology. Whatever the source of the difficulty in processing social information and in responding appropriately, this impairment gives rise to pervasive feelings of shame and inadequacy—and also then to deep feelings of depression.

Shame and social inadequacy

Shame is a response to failure and to ensuing feelings of inadequacy—especially a failure when success was expected. Such instances always involve a sense of failure in the eyes of others. The spectrum of shame-evoking failure is very wide indeed: e.g. failure to achieve academically or in a career; failure to possess a desirable accent, body, clothes, or social skills; failure to be accepted by others and be included as part of a social group; failure to understand information; failure to perceive and respond appropriately to the social requirements of a situation accurately; failure to have acquired symbols of status and social and material success; failure to retain control over display of emotion; failure to control one's body. However, the most fundamental failure, I suggest, is that of not being able to evoke an empathic response in the other. Following a hypothesis by Broucek (1979), that the sense of efficacy forms the basis of the sense of self, we might consider that one of the most basic forms of efficacy is that of being able to communicate one's needs and have them understood by the mother or other primary care-giver. This is also the case in adult life. When we are in contact with friendly others who display empathic understanding of our experience and difficulties we tend to feel relatively free of shame; we feel there is a continuity between our experience and that of others. It is when we anticipate, or actually encounter disapproval or incomprehension of our behaviour and emotions that we experience shame. At such times we feel a discontinuity or gulf between ourselves and others; we are strangers to each other.

Broucek (1991) suggests that shame may arise in the early experiences with the mother at those moments when she becomes a "stranger" to her infant. This could occur as a result of the mother's changing moods and preoccupations which may alter her behaviour and facial expression. Broucek points to the evidence of "still face" experiments (Tronick *et al.*, 1978). Interactions between mothers and three-month-old infants were filmed under two conditions; in the first, the mother was instructed to interact as she normally would; and in the second she was asked to make eye contact but not engage in facial or verbal interaction. The infants reacted to the still face first by attempting their normal engagement with the mother, but then responded either by crying in distress or by slumping down, with loss of body tonus, turning the head down and averting their gaze from the mother's face. Broucek agreed with Nathanson (1987a) that the infants showing the second kind of response were displaying an early form of shame and that this is also an aspect of the infant's *shame - produces corticosteroids, stress chemical, → induces inhibition & withdrawal — cf. sex*

response to strangers (Spitz, 1965). It is perhaps significant that the infants first attempted to engage the mother using their usual behavioural repertoire and then reacted with distress when these efforts failed. Thus the shame arose when the infant encountered an emotionally important other, the mother, who did not behave as expected, and the infant did not know how to respond to her. Suddenly the relational world was alarmingly unpredictable. It is the same with adults when our social expectations are violated—we call it embarrassment.

Schore (1998) summarizes a great deal of developmental and neurobiological data regarding facial mirroring as a major vehicle of affect communication, to conclude:

> The experience of shame is associated with unfulfilled expectations and is triggered by an appraisal of a disturbance in facial recognition, the most salient channel of non-verbal communication. [p. 65]

He sees shame arising when the young child looks to the mother for the positive emotion-generating function of facial mirroring, but finds instead a response indicating disapproval or disgust. Then, in place of the anticipated psychobiologically energized state, the child experiences shame, which is a rapidly de-energized and painful state. Whereas the child's brain in the positive emotional state of facial interaction is producing endogenous opiates that mediate pleasurable responses, in the state of shame it is generating stress biochemicals, such as corticosteroids, which induce inhibition and withdrawal. Schore suggests that shame helps the child to know when it is appropriate to withdraw and become subdued—an addition to the more commonly recognized fight–flight alternatives when faced with interpersonal threat, shame represents "para-sympathetically mediated passive coping mechanisms ... [which are] ... an alternative but equivalent strategy for effectively regulating social interactional stress" (1998, p. 72). Nathanson makes a similar point regarding the safety-seeking emotional withdrawal when a positive and familiar facial mirroring is not evoked. He describes shame as:

> a biological system by which the organism controls its affective output so that it will not remain interested or content when it may

not be safe to do so, or so that it will not remain in affective resonance with an organism that fails to match its patterns stored in memory. [1992, p. 140]

We might also consider the shame potential arising from congenital impairments of the capacity to engage in visual contact with the mother. Tantam (1991) writes:

My own hypothesis ... is that Asperger syndrome results from a failure of congenital gaze reflexes, which ensure that the normal infant attends to social signals preferentially and locks the normal infant into the ebb and flow of social interaction. The normal child, it is hypothesised, learns to anticipate how much gaze they and others merit, and this leads to the development of an "attention structure" which is shared with other people. It is from this, I argue, that social theories evolve. ... According to this hypothesis, the lack of inbuilt gaze responses results in the person with Asperger syndrome being unable to acquire the fundamentals of social competence. [p. 180]

The social awkwardness of the person with Asperger syndrome is regarded as a core feature and many aspects of this, particularly the aversion of gaze, are clearly related to shame.

Shame and guilt

It is not always easy to entirely disentangle shame from guilt. However, in general, guilt seems to be felt in response to harmful or prohibited actions or phantasies of such actions. These are often of an aggressive nature. Shame, by contrast is often to do with failures to do what is expected, and is associated with feelings of weakness. Aggression and guilt may be preferentially highlighted as a defence against feelings of weakness and shame—on the basis that it is better to feel strong and bad rather than weak. Jacobson (1965) comments that "sadistic impulses are apt to induce guilt, while masochistic, passive, dependent leanings ... tend to arouse feelings of shame and inferiority" (p. 147). She gives the following example of the interplay between shame and guilt:

This interplay frequently manifests itself in adolescent masturbation conflicts. A patient who in his adolescence suffered from compulsive

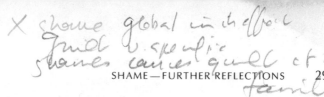

masturbation would develop intense guilt feelings about his fantasies of "raping" a girl. He would regularly ward off such sadistic impulses by indulging instead in masturbation with passive, regressive fantasies of being spoiled and sexually gratified by beautiful girls who found great pleasure in taking the sexual initiative. However, this masturbation, which would rapidly lead to orgasm, would leave him with excruciating feelings of shame and inferiority, since he regarded his fantasies—correctly—as a manifestation of his passivity, his lack of masculinity, and impotence, i.e. of his castrated self image and his unconscious passive homosexual (oral and anal) wishes. These feelings would immediately result in new impulses to prove his masculinity by "raping" girls; inducing another outburst of guilt feelings, such impulses would have to be warded off once more by passive fantasies. [p. 148]

Thus, feelings of weakness, helplessness and passivity—associated with shame—can lead to a wish to turn the tables and triumph over the other, giving rise then to feelings of guilt (Lynd, 1958). This is extremely common, since, as Gedo (1981) and G. Klein (1976) have emphasized, a major component of the developing organization of the self is the transformation of passive experience into a more active mode—to do actively what was once suffered passively and thereby move from helplessness and shame to guilt.

Some authors (e.g. Lynd, 1958; Piers & Singer, 1953) have suggested that shame is a response to failures to live up to the ego ideal, whilst guilt results from transgressions condemned by the superego. However, shame is a peculiarly global state, casting its shadow over the whole sense of self, whilst guilt tends to have a more discrete reference to particular actions (Lewis, 1971; Lynd, 1958). As Thrane (1979) puts it, in guilt we say "How can I have done *that*!"; in shame we say "How can *I* have done that!".

Shame may also give rise to guilt more directly. For example, a person might feel shame about a parent, a child, a spouse or other relative, because of their social inadequacies or behavioural peculiarities. Similar shame may be felt about one's family as a whole, especially regarding class, cultural, and educational background, leading to attitudes of awkwardness and rejection towards one's kin. This may be pronounced when a person has moved into a class or cultural group significantly different from his or her origins. Such shame about others to whom one is connected—common particularly during adolescence and early adulthood—may be experienced as an extremely painful source of guilt and feelings of disloyalty.

Shame and the look

A stand-up comedienne in therapy—Julie—talked of her contrasting experiences of being in front of an audience. When her performances went well, she would feel a wonderful intoxicating sense of agency and potency. At these times the audience would appear admiring, their responses of laughter affirming her wit and skill. This was a mirroring experience amplified to its maximum. The more responsive and engaged the audience became, the more her delivery of her material seemed to flow with effortless panache and precision of timing. On the other hand, when the audience was unresponsive, she would experience a mounting panic. Terrible feelings of shame and self-consciousness would begin to fill her whole being. Her heart would pound and her skin would feel cold. Her delivery would become increasingly hesitant and she would stumble over her words. On occasion, in response to jeers, she would actually run off the stage. At such times she did not at all feel herself to be acting from a centre of her own sense of agency, mirrored by an admiring audience, empathically responding to her humour. Instead she would feel herself to be an object of the audience's unempathic and unfriendly gaze.

Thus when the audience was responsive and clearly experiencing pleasure in her humorous communications, Julie would experience herself as a subject, an agent within her immediate interpersonal world. By contrast, when the audience appeared hostile or unresponsive, she experienced herself as an object of their scornful gaze—all sense of agency would rapidly dissipate and she would feel herself to be socially impotent. As a child she had developed a role of "performer" in the family, being funny, doing little tricks, singing etc. However, she had also experienced her mother as controlling and intrusive, preoccupied with Julie's achievements, and frequently expressing disapproval by withdrawing and presenting an icy cold demeanour. Julie described her oscillation between states of mind in which she felt herself to be in the centre of her world, into which others could be invited, and, on the other hand, states in which she felt pushed to the edge of someone else's world. In this way she described the tension, discussed by Bach (1980), between what he termed "subjective awareness", the feeling that the world is "all me", and "objective self-awareness", the sense of being there for someone else.

These patterns were apparent in the transference. Julie would complain at times of feeling treated as an object to be made sense of, rather than a person to be understood empathically from within her own subjective internal position. Interpretations, if they were not framed as an empathic grasp of her experience, but instead referred to a psychodynamic defence or process, would be experienced by her as controlling and fragmenting; at such moments she would feel objectified, shamed, and in a state of painful self-consciousness. On the other hand, she would display a marked tendency to try to fit herself into the analyst's formulations—this alternating with rebellious states in which she would fantasize wrecking the consulting room, or would fill the session with such a continuous stream of words that there was no space for the analyst to speak.

Many patients experience some degree of self-consciousness when feeling that their communications to the therapist are not immediately understood. It is as if at those times the experience is of being the object of an other's uncomprehending gaze; there is no sense of affirmation of common humanity—or of Kohut's (1984) sense of twinship, where it is felt that "here is an other who is like myself". I have also noticed that some patients who are particularly prone to self-consciousness and shame have suffered the loss of a parent or some similar catastrophe in early life. Such losses cannot easily be mourned by the young child, especially if the remaining care-givers are themselves too preoccupied with their loss, or in other ways are unable to provide empathic and responsive support. The child is likely to become withdrawn, shutting off his or her emotions, perhaps not showing outwardly much evidence of the internal devastation. Adults observing this may think with some relief that the child does not seem to be very affected. The emotional reality is that the child has been torn from the empathic matrix, feeling him/herself to be now at the centre of a cold and hostile world. What then appears to happen is that the child grows up having internalized the absence of an empathic response in the form of the *presence* of an unempathic internal object. This unempathic figure is then projected onto the therapist, leading the patient to expect a lack of understanding and responsiveness. The patient fears that he or she is gazed upon by an other who looks not with empathy but with incomprehension.

For the child, too much looking or too little looking are both damaging to the delicately emerging sense of self. The natural exhibitionism of the child looks for the "gleam in the mother's eye" (Kohut, 1971), but fears the look that seems to invade and control. Lewis (1963) describes the role of watching in a four-year-old psychotic child. The child showed a peculiar, precocious, embarrassed, self-consciousness whilst her mother demonstrated a kind of total involvement with her, constantly watching anxiously. Lewis suggests that the child seemed to have identified with the mother's watching—in this way maintaining a link to the mother, whilst at the same time affirming her own sense of self, warding off the danger of engulfment by the mother. Merleau-Ponty (1964) has described an abrupt change in the child's reactions to the look of the other. Prior to a certain point, the other's look is encouraging, but after this it becomes an embarrassment: "everything happens as though when he is looked at, his attention is displaced from the task he is carrying out to a representation of himself in the process of carrying it through".

One of the major sections of Sartre's *Being and Nothingness* dealing with shame is entitled "The look". He gives numerous examples of the phenomenology of becoming the object of the other's look:

> Let us imagine that moved by jealousy, curiosity or vice, I have just glued my ear to the door and looked through the keyhole. I am alone ... but all of a sudden I hear footsteps in the hall. Someone is looking at me! [pp. 347–349].

Sartre writes of the shock of realizing that the object of our perception can suddenly become the subject who is viewing us an the object:

> ... my apprehension of the Other in the world ... refers to the permanent possibility that a subject who sees me may be substituted for the object seen by me. [p. 345]

When we perceive the other looking at us, we cannot easily maintain that other in the position of object—we tend to feel *we* are the object:

> The Other's look hides his eyes; he seems to go *in front of them* ... to perceive is to *look at*, and to apprehend a look is not to apprehend a look-as-object in the world (unless the look is not directed upon us); it is to be conscious of *being looked at*. The look which the eyes manifest, no matter what kind of eyes they are, is a pure reference to myself. [pp. 346–347]

When we experience our self as the object for an other, we feel vulnerable and exposed:

> What I apprehend immediately when I hear the branches crackling behind me is not that *there is someone there*; it is that I am vulnerable, that I have a body which can be hurt, that I occupy a place and that I can not in any case escape from the space in which I am without defence—in short, that *I am seen.* [p. 347]

Sartre goes on to describe how our awareness of being an object for the other contains the realization that this object (this vision of one's self) that the other sees is essentially unknowable to us. The self as an object for the other is not the same as our self as the object of our own reflective consciousness:

> ... it is separated from me by a nothingness which I can not fill since I apprehend it as *not being for me* and since on principle it exists for the *Other*. Therefore I do not aim at it as if it could someday be given me but on the contrary in so far as it on principle flees from me and will never belong to me. Nevertheless *I am that Ego*; I do not reject it as a strange image, but it is present to me as a self which I *am* without *knowing* it; for I discover it in shame or pride which reveals to me the Other's look and myself at the end of that look. It is the shame or pride which makes me *live*, not *know* the situation of being looked at. [p. 350]

Sartre's examples are of the sudden reversal of the flow of consciousness, from the self-as-subject to the self-as-object (Wright, 1991). The psychologically competent adult is able to balance the subjective and objective self, so that the inner sense of agency is co-ordinated with an appropriate presentation of self to others, such that communicative behaviour is continually modified by the perceptual feedback regarding the other's view and impression of one's self (Mollon, 1993). This is the interplay of G. H. Mead's (1934) "I" and the "Me"—a balance which is necessary for the good functioning of what Lichtenberg (1983) called the "self-as-a-whole" and the "mental director". However, some people, especially those corresponding to Winnicott's (1960) account of "false self", seem to experience themselves as predominantly all "Me", excessively preoccupied with the other's image of them and quite out of touch with their "I", their own deeper feelings. Shame and feelings of embarrassed self-consciousness arise when a discrepancy becomes apparent between actual self and the presented self, or between the actual self and the image of the self that the other expects. Thus a person may feel shame when his or her grandiose aspirations are found to be discrepant with reality and this discrepancy is apparent to others. However, shame may also arise when the actual self is revealed to be discrepant with the other's image of one's self, whether this discrepancy is in a positive or negative direction; to realize that the other is underestimating one's status or achievements can evoke shame and embarrassment just as much as can finding one's achievements fall short of the other's expectations. It seems that embarrassed self-consciousness arises in the gap—in the sudden jarring disruption of the fitting together of self and other (Mollon, 1987). Indeed it is a matter of everyday observation that all instances of embarrassment involve this disruption of social expectations.

Captured by the mother's narcissism

For some children—and later adults—the threat of this "embarrassment" can be a pervasive feature of their interpersonal world, thereby becoming internalized as a core component of the personality. This occurs when the mother is experienced as excessively controlling and demanding, requiring her child to fulfil *her* narcissistic needs whilst the child's own exhibitionism and phase-appropriate grandiosity are neglected. The pressure on the child is then to fit in with the mother's narcissism and to deny his or her own developmental initiatives. To some extent this corresponds to the situation described by Winnicott (1960) in his discussion of true and false self. However, it is articulated in more detail in Kohut's (1971) account of the vertical split in certain narcissistic developments.

For example, Kohut describes the case of Mr J, whose presentation in the analysis was for some time characterized by qualities of grandiosity and exhibitionism. During one session he mentioned casually that after shaving in the mornings he would carefully rinse his razor and clean the sink before washing and drying his face. It was not immediately apparent why Mr J spoke of this and why he felt it to be important, but Kohut observed that it was recounted in a somewhat arrogant and tense fashion. In retrospect Kohut began to see that this was an early indication of a hidden area in Mr J's personality derived from a combination of vertical and horizontal splits—such that one vertically split sector was an expression of his accommodation to his mother's narcissism whilst another sector contained his conscious depression and his own *repressed* grandiose–exhibitionistic strivings. They gradually arrived at an understanding of how Mr J's overt vanity and arrogance was linked to his mother's praise for various of his performances in which he was shown off for the enhancement of her self-esteem. Thus, in the example of the shaving routine, Mr J was displaying himself as a "good boy who leaves the sink nice and clean", a quality that presumably would have gained his mother's approval. However, his fastidious washing of the razor and basin took precedence over attention to his face. Kohut saw this as an endopsychic replica of his need for his mother's acceptance of his displayed body self *and her rejection of this*. He explains that Mr J's apparent grandiosity and exhibitionism was not truly his own:

> This noisily displayed grandiose–exhibitionistic sector of his personality had occupied throughout his life the conscious centre of the psychic stage. Yet it was not fully real to him, provided no lasting satisfaction, and remained split off from the coexisting, more centrally located sector of his psyche in which he experienced those vague depressions coupled with shame and hypochondria that had motivated him to seek psychoanalytic help. [1971, pp. 180–181]

Kohut here describes a situation in which the child's narcissism and exhibitionism is essentially *hijacked* by the mother's narcissism, so that the exhibitionistic display is essentially hers. The analytic task, as Kohut sees it, is to locate the patient's authentic narcissistic needs, which are kept in check (unconscious) by intense feelings of shame:

> Gradually, and against strong resistances (motivated by deep shame, fear of overstimulation, fear of traumatic disappointment), the narcissistic transference began to centre around his need to have his body–mind–self confirmed by the analyst's admiring acceptance. [p. 182]

Kohut and Mr J eventually came to understand that a crucial fear was that the analyst would value the patient only as a vehicle for his own aggrandizement and would reject him if he displayed his own initiatives—a transference pattern that precisely repeated his childhood anxieties in relation to his mother. Mr J's overt grandiosity and exhibitionism had been expressed through one side of a vertically split personality, whilst his own authentic narcissistic needs, linked with shame, had been held in repression (horizontal split) within the other vertically split sector (Kohut represents this in a diagram on p. 179 of *The Analysis of the Self*, showing a combination of vertical and horizontal splitting). As Mr J's wishes to display his "grandiose–exhibitionistic body self" were identified and worked through in the transference, Mr J was able to arrive at a point where, as he humorously put it, he could "prefer my face to the razor"!

The background of a mother who required the child to function as an extension of herself, in such a way that there was no room for the child's own separate self, does seem to be common with patients who are prone to painful self-consciousness. In such cases the child appears to have colluded with this need in the mother, often because the reward was to remain in a special or privileged position in relation to the mother. This might be so particularly if the mother denigrated the father, so that the child felt preferred to the figure who would otherwise have been the Oedipal rival. In these circumstances, the real rival for the mother's love is not the father but the *false image that the mother has of the child*. It is the dilemma portrayed in Oscar Wilde's novel, *The Picture of Dorian Gray* (B. Green, 1979). The picture, the image, is loved and it this that Dorian wishes to swap places with. By contrast, the unseen and unmirrored self becomes increasingly degenerate, its features distorted by envy, represented by the hideously deteriorating picture hidden in the attic. Once the child has made this devil's pact of identifying with

Very hold: the o. mind is not the child itself (which will be postlement) and the m.'s image of the child, Then it very annihilation of self? make the person desperate

the image that mother loves, sacrificing his or her true self in the service of retaining her love, the hidden corrosive inner development is then set on its inevitable course. With the possibility of authentic development thus sabotaged, the person will feel that the true inner self is increasingly unlovable and must remain hidden. The ensuing shame and rage may be intense and profound— erupting sometimes later in life in seemingly incomprehensible self-destructive acts of sabotage of the person's achievements (and sometimes actual suicide). In such cases the destruction is an unconscious attempt to break free of the prison of the false self and the mother's narcissism (even if by destruction of the body).

Shame and exhibitionism

> Historically we have castigated the psychological exhibitionist ... It seems to me that we have become excessively narrow-minded in our thinking to imagine that the art of being seen, being observed, being noticed, being appreciated and so forth, should be confined to the celebrity or exhibitionist. Surely, in an emotionally literate society, everybody needs to be taken seriously, and we ought to endeavour to provide room so that each and every one of us can have an arena. [Kahr, 2001, pp. 65–66]

Some degree of shame is commonly associated with exposure to the view of others, even if that view is favourable (Buss, 1980). Compliments commonly evoke embarrassment. Darwin (1872) noted that an attractive young woman might blush if a man gazes at her, even though she knows that his look is admiring. This shame-shyness relating to pleasurable aspects of exhibitionism is quite normal. For some, however, conflicts over exhibitionism can be excruciatingly painful.

A young woman complained of social inhibitions and "paranoia" when amongst a crowd of people. She feared that everyone would be looking at her critically and judging her. Analysis revealed that behind this fear lay a strong exhibitionist desire. She wanted to be the focus of admiring attention. It emerged that when she had been younger she had become used to such admiration, being an only child, and adored by her mother (her father having been absent as a result of divorce). Her fantasies were of being a wonderful singer and dancer—of performing on stage to rapturous acclaim. The problem was that she felt her actual achievements did not match up to her ambitions. Therefore her exhibitionism caused her intense anxiety. It overstimulated her, evoking a fear of crude exhibitionistic display that was not harnessed to talent and achievement worthy of admiration. Her difficulty was self-reinforcing, since her conflicts over exhibitionism gave rise to intense shame, which was the root of her social anxieties, and thereby inhibited her from developing her actual talent as a singer and also prevented her from gaining other work achievements that could provide a realistic basis for self-esteem.

In another case, a patient reported that as a young boy he had frequently been used as a child performer in variety shows—his mother being keenly involved in local amateur dramatics. The boy had not chosen to undertake these performances at his own initiative and in fact experienced intense anxiety before going on stage—especially since he was, by temperament, rather shy. However, his mother had been dismissive of his expressions of anxiety, thereby teaching him to disregard his own signals of shame. Moreover, he did not have any particular talent to display on stage and the "performances" consisted essentially of the amusement value of a small boy dressed in a costume illustrating a popular song of the day—such as a "jailbird" outfit to accompany "jail house rock", which he would then pretend to sing. In retrospect, it was possible to understand that the boy's exhibitionism had been overstimulated by this abnormal exposure to a large and seemingly admiring audience. What exacerbated the problem, however, was that his mother caused the performances to continue well past an age when they were at all appropriate, and when the boy could clearly sense that he was no longer regarded as "cute" and the audience was no longer unequivocally admiring. In particular, his peer group became overtly mocking. The boy grew up to be a man with a marked proneness to shame and social anxiety.

These examples correspond to situations described by Kohut (1971), in which the child's natural exhibitionism had been either overstimulated or excessively suppressed. As a result, the exhibitionism would be repressed. It would not then have the opportunity to transmute gradually into more mature modified forms that are grounded in socially approved achievement. Remaining thus infantile and crude in quality, the desire to exhibit—to "show off" —would be feared unconsciously as very threatening. The potential flooding of the psyche with unmodified infantile exhibitionism can be a source of overwhelming shame. In most of Kohut's examples, the father was absent, as in the case of the woman described above. The resulting position (of too much mother and too little father) may mean a failure to progress into the triadic Oedipal position, leaving the child insufficiently differentiated from the mother and with an uncertain sense of self; this can be a crucial component of excessive shame-proneness (Mollon, 1993).

Shame and the body

A shame prone patient would frequently speak of his wish to be "pure intellect", to be without a body with its needs, its lusts, and its imperfections. He was critical of the appearance of his own body and those of others, especially that of his girlfriend. It was apparent that part of his unconscious hope had been that psychoanalysis would help him achieve a state of enduring rationality and a triumph of intellect over body. His body was a source of great shame. It represented limitations and biological need—a continual affront to narcissistic aspirations for freedom, perfection, and self-sufficiency. Andre Green, in a discussion of "moral narcissism" writes:

> In the case of the moral narcissist, hell is not other people— narcissism has eliminated them—but rather the body. The body is an Other, resurrected in spite of numerous attempts to wipe out its traces. The body is a limitation, a servitude, a termination ... their body is their absolute master—their shame. [1982]

The moral narcissist condemns the body and its appetites. It is an attitude close to the "profound asceticism of adolescence" described by Anna Freud (1966), adolescence being a time of particular proneness to shame. Green relates moral narcissism to circumstances similar to those Winnicott describes as leading to the development of false self, where the mother's agenda to have a particular kind of child prevails over the child's own initiatives. He

The body exists for the Other. The body is the Other. Body belongs to M-other

40   SHAME AND JEALOUSY

suggests that the omnipotence attributed to the mother may be reinforced if it is associated with the mother's desire to bear a child without the contribution of the father. Many patients who are particularly shame prone do seem to have had mothers who were rather controlling and who devalued the father (Mollon, 1993).

Sartre also describes the way the body can be felt to betray the self insofar as it exists for the other:

> "To feel oneself blushing", "to feel oneself sweating" etc., are inaccurate expressions which the shy person uses to describe his state; what he really means is that he is physically and constantly conscious of his body, not as it is for him but as it is *for the other*. This constant uneasiness which is the apprehension of my body's alienation as irremediable can determine ... a pathological fear of blushing; these are nothing but a horrified metaphysical apprehension of the existence of my body for the Other. We often say that the shy man is "embarrassed by his own body". Actually this is incorrect; I cannot be embarrassed by my own body as I exist it. It is my body as it is for the Other which may embarrass me. [1956, pp. 462–463]

The original Other is of course the mother—and in shame-prone people, the body has been felt to belong to *her*, and is therefore the object of hatred.

A particular area of shame in relation to the body concerns sexuality. Certain German terms illustrate the close association of shame and sexuality. For example, the genital region is called *die Scham*, the pubic mound *Schamberg* and pubic hair *Schambaare*. There is something about sexuality that is inherently intimate to the self (and one's lover) and which cannot be shared publicly without some feeling of shame—or if there is an absence of shame we feel something important is missing. When I was first training in psychoanalytic therapy I was taught that it was very important to ask a patient about masturbation fantasies during the initial assessment because these were considered to provide clues to crucial conflicts and anxieties. I have always tended to feel reluctant to make such enquiries, especially in an initial meeting. Although it does seem that masturbation fantasies can reveal core desires and anxieties relating to essential aspects of the self, to ask about these directly (unless done with the utmost tact) can be experienced as violating and in disregard of the patient's natural shame. This is especially the case insofar as sexual fantasies can often be understood as sexualized narratives about injuries and vulnerabilities in the sense of self—the core self that must not be violated, as Winnicott (1960), Khan (1972), Stoller (1976) and Kohut (1971, 1977) amongst others have emphasized.

Some analysts seem inclined to assume that shame associated with masturbation must be to do with the content of the accompanying phantasies. I do not believe this is necessarily the case. One patient, Jeanette, reported, with tremendous embarrassment, how she had learned to masturbate and give herself an orgasm at the age of seven and had indulged regularly in this over the subsequent years, but always feeling some sense of shame afterwards. Her turning to her own body for pleasurable stimulation had been given impetus partly by her feelings of loneliness and lack of emotional stimulation—her lone parent mother tending to be preoccupied and often intoxicated. One day, whilst at school aged 14, Jeanette had experienced a sudden "realization" of the nature of her sexual activities and was overwhelmed with intense feelings of shame and a terror that others would know her secret. She had rushed home and tried to tell her mother, who failed to respond in an empathic manner but instead reacted with anxiety and disapproval. Subsequently Jeanette developed a disabling social anxiety, which turned out to be based on the fear that the word "masturbation" would crop up in conversation and that she would go red; naturally her anxiety about blushing and this being seen tended to bring about the very effect she feared whenever a conversation turned to sexual matters. Jeanette's adult feelings of shame centred not only on her childhood masturbation, which she regarded as excessive, but also on her view of herself as having an abnormal interest in sex. Discussion of her sexuality in psychotherapy led to a rapid diminution in her feelings of shame and associated anxiety.

The sexual stimulation of one's own body can be experienced as a private addiction, associated with feelings of weakness and thus shame. Its prominence in a person's life may be felt to be an indication of his or her inadequacy and inability to form a satisfying sexual relationship with another person. An activity of giving pleasure to oneself, which inherently is non-social and private,

X O/D - *unce inguity*
sexl. fantacy "1 q nei
intense
pleasure

42   SHAME AND JEALOUSY

inevitably must be associated with shame if it is exposed to others. Masturbation is the only pleasurable activity that, inherent in its nature, is not for sharing with others.

Sexuality has many functions—obviously including procreation and the communication of love and intimacy—but it also often appears associated with the sense of autonomy and identity (Lichtenstein, 1961). Injuries to the sense of self and its autonomy, suffered in the early relationship with the mother, may give rise to sexual behaviours and fantasies that have the unconscious function of denying the anxiety and injury, asserting the survival of the self (Stoller, 1976). Through the unconscious ingenuity of sexual fantasy the deepest anxiety about the viability of the psychological–bodily self is transformed into the source of the most intense pleasure.

Parents often do interfere with the child's autonomy in relation to its exploration of the body's sexuality. Amsterdam and Levitt (1980) suggest that a common source of painful embarrassed self-consciousness is the negative reaction of a parent who looks anxiously or disapprovingly when the child is engaged in genital exploration or play. They argue that the mother's disapproval of the child's autoerotic exploration may be one of the first narcissistic injuries experienced by the child. Amsterdam and Levitt point out that, in contrast to the "gleam in the mother's eye" which Kohut (1971) emphasized as a foundation of the child's sense of self, mothers in our culture do not normally beam whilst their infants play with themselves. They argue that in this way the child's dream of his or her own perfection is destroyed and the source of pleasure—his or her own bodily sensations—now produce shame. Exploration of sexuality has led the child out of the Garden of Eden.

Shame and depression

Guilt, rather than shame, has tended to be emphasized as one of the crucial affects (along with anger) in states of depression. However, if one listens to the preoccupations of depressed patients, it is not difficult to discern repetitive ruminations over shameful and narcissistically injurious events. Indeed, the characteristics of the "depressive personality", as described by such authors as Rado (1928), Fenichel (1946) and Arieti and Bemporad (1980)—narcissistic vulnerability, sensitivity to slights, insults, criticisms and disappointments—may all be seen in terms of proneness to shame. Certainly depression is, in part, a narcissistic disturbance, since the disruption in the sense of self and in self-esteem is quite central (Mollon & Parry, 1984).

Whilst depression is often a response to loss, what is not always appreciated fully is the role of the shame and humiliation inherent in the loss. When a relationship ends, there is the pain of loss of the other person, but in addition, for the one who is rejected, there is a narcissistic injury—the feelings of shame, humiliation, and injury to self-esteem. It is common for some people consistently to avoid receiving such an injury by ensuring that they are always the ones who end the relationship—becoming "serial rejecters", agents of narcissistic trauma inflicted on others who are left to suffer the ensuing depression.

Rejection brings shame. Shame evokes rage and hatred of the self that is the object of shame. Self-esteem plummets. A state of depression descends. In such a state, the person feels even more undesirable and unlovable. Shame, rage, self-hatred, falling self-esteem, depression, and further shame—this tangle of "breakdown products" of narcissistic injury (Kohut, 1977)—spiral relentlessly in an accelerating negative feedback, culminating, in the case of vulnerable individuals, in suicide or serious self-harm. Such individuals know that their deteriorating mental state makes them increasingly unattractive and undesirable and this adds to their sense of shame. Shame begets shame—and the only antidote to shame is the empathic and affectionate response of another person. Those who are fortunate enough to have experienced sufficient love and empathy in childhood are able to draw upon these internalized experiences and find their own self-directed empathy. For those who have not, shame may expand without limit.

Some people who are prone to depression live under the oppression of a harsh and shame-inducing superego (Cohen *et al.*, 1954; Morrison, 1989b) derived from experiences with very demanding and status-conscious parents. In childhood these people found that failure or rebellion led to withdrawal of love. The adult pattern may often then be that of an alternation between compliance with the demands of the internalized parental figures and states of manic rebellion. For example, one young woman had grown up within a particular ethnic culture in which females were expected to behave with extreme inhibition and modesty; she would go for long periods in conformity with these expectations, but periodically would enter manic phases in which she would reject her traditional clothing and become sexually adventurous and promiscuous; this manic phase would then end with a crash into depression and overwhelming feelings of shame about her preceding behaviour. In addition to her feelings of shame for herself, she would feel she had brought shame upon her family.

To some extent the active destructiveness directed towards the self displayed by certain depressive patients can be understood as an attempt to avoid feelings of helplessness and shame in response to rejection. Guntrip (1968) made a similar point when he argued that sado–masochistic internal object relations function as a defence against intolerable feelings of weakness and helplessness. In such a way, depression can be seen sometimes as an attempt to protect the sense of self (Mollon & Parry, 1984). For example, one chronically depressed patient had never managed to separate from her mother, with whom she maintained a hostile masochistic dependence. She described how all her life she had felt she had to be something for other people, whether they be mother, friends, or the therapist in the transference; she felt she always had to slot into the "vision" that her mother had for her. This became quite explicit in the transference where she felt that to become dependent on the therapist meant that she would be taken over and would lose all her autonomy. She made several plans for suicide, which she saw as one way in which she could escape from the grip of the other and affirm her own self even if this meant her death. In this way she could assert that her life belonged to her and was therefore hers to end. Each time she made these plans she threw out all her personal possessions and letters and anything that had any emotional meaning for her. Eventually she became able to say why she did this. It was, she said, in order to prevent others prying into her personal belongings after she was dead. Thus she wished to avoid the sense of shame associated with violation of her core self, even after death. She was engaged in a lifelong struggle to emerge from the shame-ridden state of being an object for the other, and to find and protect the autonomy and integrity of her self—even at the expense of ending the life of her body.

Embarrassment about the self

It will be apparent from the discussion so far that for those who are prone to shame, the fundamental embarrassment is the self. For example, Mr D wished to be "all things to all men". He would adapt his manner, voice, opinions, tastes etc. according to whom he was with. In this way he endeavoured to hide his real self. His greatest fear was that his self would embarrassingly emerge from its camouflage—that he would say or do something that was not in keeping with the image he was attempting to present. A chameleon, he was continually afraid that his colours might not match his surroundings. Naturally, Mr D's real self was hidden from "himself". He did not know what he really thought or felt or desired—but he feared that something from these hidden areas might leak out, catastrophically breaking the carefully constructed blending with the other person(s). Moreover, he feared being exposed as a fraud. He was not sure exactly in what way he was a fraud, but he sensed that his whole way of presenting himself in the world was fraudulent. He would always agree with whatever the analyst said—including interpretations about his false self. The problem was that he genuinely did not know the content of what lay behind his false presentation—he simply feared that whatever it was would embarrassingly break out. In this way his entire being was pervaded by the fear of shame and embarrassment.

Shame and rage

Whilst one common reaction to shame is a wish to withdraw and hide, another is rage. This is a violent attack on the persons or circumstances that have brought about a humiliation. Kohut (1972) wrote an important paper about shame-based narcissistic rage, which he described as follows:

> Narcissistic rage occurs in many forms; they all share, however, a specific psychological flavour which gives them a distinct position within the wide realm of human aggressions. The need for revenge, for righting a wrong, for undoing a hurt by whatever means, and a deeply anchored, unrelenting compulsion in the pursuit of all these aims, which gives no rest to those who have suffered a narcissistic

injury—these are the characteristic features of narcissistic rage in all its forms and which set it apart from other kinds of aggression. [p. 638]

Kohut gives the example of a patient who would skilfully but subtly embarrass and humiliate acquaintances at social gatherings by introducing some aspect of their national or religious background, avowedly in the spirit of being very open and liberal. Gradually, in the course of analysis, he became aware of "an erotically tinged excitement" at these moments of the victim's embarrassment and his underlying sadism became clear. This led to his recall of recurrent experiences of shame and rage in his childhood. In addition to ridiculing and criticizing him in public, his mother had insisted on regularly exposing and inspecting his genitals, ostensibly in order to find out whether he had masturbated. As a result he had formed vengeful sadistic fantasies, now enacted in his cruel exposures of his social victims to the gaze of others.

Narcissistic rage is often not subtle at all. The ostracized loner who engages in a school shooting; terrorist attacks by groups who feel disempowered and excluded from world prosperity; the rise of Nazi Germany after the humiliations of the defeat in the first world war—all these and many others readily come to mind as examples.

Narcissistic vulnerability (Mollon, 1986) and chronic narcissistic rage derive from childhood experiences of humiliation and failures to evoke empathic understanding from care-givers. Kohut draws attention to Ruth Benedict's study of narcissistic rage amongst the Japanese, which she attributes to methods of childrearing based on ridicule and threats of ostracism. Benedict describes how:

> sometimes people explode in the most aggressive acts. They are often roused to these aggressions not when their principles or their freedom is challenged ... but when they detect an insult or a detraction. [1946, p. 293]

Kohut links narcissistic rage to the "catastrophic reaction" sometimes shown by brain injured patients when faced with an incapacity to perform a task that normally would be easily accomplished—for example, when an aphasic patient is unable to name a familiar object. This incapacity is clearly a source of shame—and is particularly humiliating since, as Kohut points out, we tend to experience our thought processes as belonging to the core of our self. He compares this to a similar, albeit milder, version of the same incapacity when we make a slip of the tongue. Some patients, he suggests, experience slips of the tongue and other expressions of the unconscious as narcissistic blows and in response "are enraged about the sudden exposure of their lack of omnipotence in the area of their own mind". Indeed, Freud (1901), in his original discussion of slips of the tongue, noted that these are often followed by "a trace of affect" which "is clearly in the nature of shame" (p. 83).

I have often found that when a patient becomes enraged in psychotherapy or analysis, it is because he or she feels that the analyst is not accurately (empathically) grasping their experience; instead, the analyst is perceived as persisting in a point of view of their own. It becomes a battle of perspectives. Similarly, I may find myself experiencing some degree of "rage" towards a patient if I feel that he or she is not listening to what I am actually saying but is persisting in misperceiving and mishearing my meaning according to their own assumptions. The process is one I have described as "identity imposition", an insistence on viewing a person in a particular way, despite contrary evidence (Mollon, 2001a). It can be a pervasive part of some people's childhood experience, sowing the seeds of chronic narcissistic rage—and, of course, they will then be inclined to want to turn the tables and subject others (including the analyst or therapist) to the same experience.

Adaptive and maladaptive functions of shame

Although extreme shame can be devastating, leaving a psychic wasteland in which all traces of self-esteem are obliterated, the emerging field of evolutionary psychology (e.g. Buss, 1999) teaches that all basic emotions (including shame and guilt) must have some adaptive function. A person without shame would encounter difficulties in relation to others. He or she might engage in behaviour that violates group norms and leads to social exclusion, thereby losing the support and protection of the group and wider society. Access to resources and to potential mates might then be reduced; evolutionary pressures would therefore have selected shame for its advantage in facilitating reproductive success (Greenwald & Harder, 1998).

PTO Evolutionary Psychology : shame was a function — reproductive cycle. Pines — an adaptive social function

Shame is a means by which society maintains its own norms and values. It is a signal of violation of these. Pines (1995) comments:

shamed the gp

> Shame protects our own integrity and tells us if we have been invaded and exploited as well as telling us that we have failed to earn our self-respect, and therefore feel exposed to and invaded by the higher aspects to which we aspire. Guilt will tell us that we have damaged others and that we can expect retaliation or punishment. Both shame and guilt are social markers essential to finding our positions in family and in all subsequent groups. Shame and guilt teach us through painful but inevitable trial and error how to adapt ourselves to social roles and how to influence others to adapt to us. We learn when and how and how much to be open to others: how to manage appropriate closeness and distance: how not to hurt or be hurt: modesty, tact, social sensitivity and sympathy are all learnt this way. And we learn to be human by knowing that what we feel others also feel. [pp. 350–351]

VITAL for OD

It is through a sensitivity to shame in others that we can show social kindness, minimizing the potential for our fellow human beings to feel embarrassed, inadequate, awkward, left out, and so on. Social intercourse always hovers on the edge of potential shame and embarrassment, since the possibilities of misunderstandings, misperceptions, and misjudgements are ever-present. The absence of feelings of shame can be taken as a signal of being "at home", amongst friends, and of belonging to the group; one might say that "love is not having to feel shame"!

Some individuals are insensitive to signals of shame with the consequence that they are repeatedly ostracized without fully realizing why and how this occurs. This may occur either through social dyslexia or as a result of an active repudiation, or bypassing (Lewis, 1971) of shame signals because of excessive shame in childhood. Certain kinds of narcissistic disturbance (Bateman, 1998; Kernberg, 1975; Kohut, 1971; Rosenfeld, 1987), may be based in this combination of extreme shame-proneness and insensitivity to shame signals (Harder, 1984). In manic states of mind, a person may become disinhibited, triumphantly disregarding social norms and signals of social disapproval, as well as the internalized shame-based prohibitions of childhood (Morrison, 1989b). When the manic state has passed, the person may suffer terrible shame on recolecting his or her *shameless* earlier behaviour. The repudiation of shame signals may also give rise to paranoid states (Meissner, 1986); rather than experiencing shame (and associated feelings of weakness, defectiveness, or inadequacy) directly, the person experiences feelings of persecution by others. Shame signals are readily externalized in this way since their origin is external and based in the responses of others.

Conformity to group norms can, of course, be harmful if the group is delinquent or destructive. Fears of shame in relation to a peer group can lead an adolescent into drug addiction or other self-damaging and antisocial behaviour that is in conflict with internal morality— thus leading to feelings of guilt. Paradoxically, some groups value a repudiation of shame and an embracing of shameless and socially rebellious behaviour; the result then is shame about feelings of shame. Much of the proto-Nazi philosophy of Nietzsche can be understood as a relentless war against shame (Wurmser, 1999).

The social function of shame gives a clue to something profoundly disconcerting at the heart of the human experience—a haunting paradox hinted at in much of Lacan's writings.[1] We can feel shame if we are revealed to be in some respect an imposter— claiming an identity that we do not have. However, there is a way in which all human identities are false insofar as they are derived from culture (Mollon, 2001a). We all must construct our "identity" out of the roles, images, and language available within the culture into which we are born—and especially within a particular family within the culture. Human beings do not exist outside human culture—but culture is highly variable and plastic. All selves are illusory "false selves"—no matter how vigorously and sometimes violently they might be defended—formed out of this plastic and elusive substance that pre-exists us and yet continually evolves. The threat of shame in its social function binds us to the group, to the culture—and to the illusion. But there is always the threat—a barely perceptible dread—that the illusion will unravel.

Summary

Shame can be distinguished from guilt, the latter being more specific and usually related to aggression and transgression, whilst shame relates more to feelings of inadequacy. There can be complicated spirals of interaction between shame and guilt, as shame leads to rage and aggression—the wish to do actively to others what was suffered passively—which leads to guilt, which may be warded off by a retreat to passivity, which leads to further shame, and so on.

Shame can be associated with a very fundamental kind of social inadequacy—a sense of not fitting in, of not being able to enter the dance of human discourse—and can be illustrated in an extreme form in some instances of schizophrenia. A fundamental sense of inadequacy may be felt by the small child who fails to evoke an empathic response from the mother. Facial mirroring between infant and mother is an important vehicle of transmission of affect, having a direct effect on the developing child's brain. The "still face" experiments indicate that an absence of the expected facial mirroring can be extremely disturbing to the infant, provoking primitive shame responses. Shame is, in other ways too, intimately associated with looking and being looked at. A distinction can be drawn between the look of empathy, which affirms the looked-at person as subject, and the look which objectifies and creates shame. The work of Sartre and of social theorists, such as G. H. Mead, are relevant here. Links can also be made with psychoanalytic concepts of false self, where the being-for-the-other takes precedence over being-for-self. Embarrassment occurs in disrupted expectations that one person has of an other—thus the "true self" can be an embarrassment when it conflicts with the "false self" or with the image that the other has of one's self.

Shame is also associated with conflicts over exhibitionism. This natural wish to display the self to others can be subject to criticism or to overstimulation, resulting in its repression; there is then a chronic fear of crude exhibitionism breaking out in a destabilizing manner—a situation particularly described by Kohut. Another personality constellation described by Kohut is one in which the child's exhibitionism has, so to speak, been hijacked by the mother, so that his or her performance is for the mother's benefit; the child's "own" exhibitionism is repressed and associated with shame.

Shame is intimately associated with sexuality, which is also linked to the sense of self, of privacy, and of autonomy. Masturbation, regardless of the content of associated fantasies, is linked with shame. It is a form of pleasure that inherently is asocial. Parents often express disapproval of children's masturbation, causing a significant narcissistic blow, a thwarting of the child's developing sense of autonomy, and an increase in painful self-consciousness and shame.

Depressed patients are often suffering from hidden shame, struggling with the impact of narcissistic injuries. Suicidal pre-occupations may express a desire to assert autonomy—to retake possession of one's life by ending it. Manic states express a rebellion against shame. Experiences that evoke shame are also likely to evoke rage—sometimes termed "narcissistic rage". This can be a significant feature of the aggression found in depressive states of mind.

The field of evolutionary psychology teaches that shame must have adaptive functions. The signal of shame serves to maintain group cohesion, which helps to promote inclusive reproductive fitness and ensure the protection of the community. Some forms of personality disturbance involve a failure to read shame signals, either due to an inability to do so or an active repudiation of shame. This can lead to paranoid states. Shame promotes identification with the group/family/culture—and yet all human identities are illusory and all selves are "false selves"—a paradox that means the threat of shame is ever-present and is structured into the human condition.

Note

1. Lacan's own work is often difficult for the non-French reader to understand. One of the best introductions, in my view, is by Gurewich (1999). She outlines Lacan's insight into the illusory sense of self or subjectivity inherent in the human condition. The child is shaped by social, cultural and linguistic forms that are originally external but are woven into the developing "subject":

> From structuralism Lacan borrows the idea that the individual does not start his career in the world as a subject but becomes shaped by structural forces that are not graspable phenomenologically. ... The fact that we believe we are the sole engineers of our thoughts and feelings, that we believe we are autonomous and cohesive individuals in control

of out actions, that we think we know why we seek analytic treatment, that we imagine that the analyst knows something about us that we don't know, that we feel that the analyst is casting judgement upon us— these aspects of experience are what Lacan calls *méconaissance* or misrecognition. This *méconaissance*—our usual way of being in the world—gives us access only to a realm of illusion ... [p. 7]

CHAPTER THREE

Psychic murder syndrome

S ometimes the mother's rejection of the child's communicative initiatives, and of his or her needs for understanding and empathy are so profound that the developing self is pervaded with shame and distrust. In such cases the natural wish to make emotional connection with others is thrown partly into reverse. The core self is covered by various levels of (unconscious) disguise and protection against overwhelming shame. A resulting pattern of sabotage of intimate attachment relationships can appear perplexingly destructive, unless the underlying process and motive are understood.

The "Stepford Child"

I have noticed the following constellation of features occurring frequently in patients who have experienced their early environment as fundamentally opposed to their authentic self potential. This psychological environment was perceived as intent on "psychic murder"—wanting to do away with the child's actual self and replace it with an alternative preferred version. An analogy can be drawn with the film "Stepford Wives", in which the sinister "men's club" kill the wives and create artificial replicas that look identical to the original, except that the new versions are completely compliant with their husbands' desires; here we might think of a "Stepford Child". The mother of such a child may have been experienced as extremely controlling, invasive, and lacking in empathy. This would be associated with pervasive shame, both because the child's need to be understood empathically would be continually thwarted, and because the core self would be felt to be in danger of violation. As a result, the child would come to feel that attachment relationships are fundamentally threatening to the core self. In later life, the formation of attachment, involving potential vulnerability, would give rise to anxiety. The stronger the attachment, the greater the anxiety.

In women, this pattern may be associated with promiscuity, combined with sexual inhibition within the main attachment relationship. This is because sex within an attachment relationship is experienced as violation, modelled on the original perception of the mother as invasive and controlling. Sex with the attachment partner is felt to be abusive and an imposition. Any hint of pressure or expectation of compliance with the partner's desire would evoke intense resistance to sexual activity. The woman may be able to express her sexuality and achieve gratification only with a partner to whom she is not attached, or by masturbation. By these means, her sense of agency and autonomy in relation to her sexuality is preserved. This protection is of considerable importance since sexuality—resting on a knife-edge between shame and pride—inherently connotes privacy and intimacy with the core self.

Deleting the message

The person who has experienced psychic murder early in life will be determined that this should never happen again. Accordingly, he or she will identify with the "murderer" and will continually kill off potential relationships. The unconscious principle here is that it is better to end the relationship and kill off the emotion actively than to suffer this passively as the one who is abandoned or emotionally destroyed. For example, a patient, Jennifer, described how she would often scornfully rebuff advances from men, especially if they seemed to want anything more emotionally intimate than sex. She spoke with a certain sadistic glee of having received a number of text messages from a man who was obviously interested in her. She did not know who the man was—and nor did she appear to feel any curiosity to find out by responding to his messages. She took particular pleasure in deleting them all, mostly without even reading them. Some time later, the man began another flurry of text messages. This time she did reply to one of them, resulting in further correspondence and a dinner invitation. She became terrified that she had allowed herself to be vulnerable and experienced a strong impulse to break off the relationship before it had developed. Her behaviour of deleting the text messages, before even reading them, could be taken as a vivid metaphor for her sadistic and triumphant elimination of emotional connections before they can be registered. In part it was her own attachment-seeking emotional self that she sadistically thwarted.

As her activity of psychic murder was interpreted, Jennifer began to reflect upon a pattern such that the length she allowed a relationship to last varied in accord with how loving and decent the man was—the one who had been most loving lasted a year, whilst the one who had been "a complete bastard" lasted four years. She spoke of how she would consciously tell herself that a relationship with a man who was abusive towards her should not be continued, but she had nevertheless stuck with it, in contrast with her rejection of men who were loving and reliable. In the light of an understanding of the overall syndrome she began to recognize that the unconscious thought was "an abusive relationship is preferable to a loving one because it is less dangerous and it does not matter if it ends". The basic problem here is that love cannot be trusted because the original object of love—the mother—was experienced as both loving (in maintaining the child's physical life) whilst being murderous towards the child's psyche and personality.

Gradually, the picture that emerged of Jennifer's mother was of a woman who preferred to live within a pretence based on an image of how she thought a family and a mother–daughter relationship should be. On reminiscing about Jennifer's childhood, she would refer to family activities, as if in support of the image of a happy household—but these recollections, although correct in a literal

sense, were completely at odds with the emotional reality experienced by Jennifer, of a family pervaded by rows and little real
communication. Jennifer described having never felt emotionally
understood by either of her parents. This was a continuing source of
great pain and rage.

The murder of relationships can also take place in relation to the
child of the person with this syndrome. For example, after I had
pointed out the process of psychic murder to Jennifer, she began to
tell me with considerable anxiety and embarrassment that when her
babies were young she often experienced an impulse to smother
them in order to prevent them suffering the pain inherent in life and
relationships. Even now that they were grown up, she would
sometimes worry they might be killed in an accident, and then
console herself with the thought that they would thereby be spared
further potential pain. Another patient who had left her husband
and young son decided that it would be best to tell her child that she
had died—a rather radical form of killing the relationship. It is not
that such a mother perpetrates psychic murder on her own child—
by being invasive and controlling etc.—but the child, representing
the mother's own vulnerable potential self, may thus provoke the
same murderous impulses that are experienced internally. Such
mothers do not actually murder their children, and are often
extremely caring and devoted as mothers, but the *idea* of murder
may be there.

Naturally, psychic murder will be regularly manifest in the
transference. Jennifer would often experience thoughts of breaking
off the therapy. She would also delay setting off for her session until
the very last moment, or even later, feeling very reluctant to come.
Once the psychic murder syndrome was interpreted to her, she
began to experience an intense eagerness to attend. A pattern
apparent with other patients is that periods of emotional contact
and psychological work, experienced as rewarding and encouraging to the analyst, may be followed by a seeming destruction of the
apparent progress, resulting in the analyst feeling profoundly
discouraged. This negative therapeutic reaction should not be
understood as an expression of envy, but as a predictable function
of the defences inherent in the psychic murder syndrome.

A further feature of the syndrome is that some of the emotional
components of the attachment relationship may be blocked from

awareness. This is part of the same process of killing off vulnerability. To be attached and vulnerable is felt to be very dangerous.
Emotions involving potential pain are therefore "murdered" at birth.
This applies only within the attachment relationship, however;
emotions in other contexts may be fully available. Because emotions
are often blocked from emerging into consciousness, they may be
expressed purely physiologically in somatic symptoms. Generalized
non-specific anxiety and somatic tension may at times be the
predominant forms of emotion. The blocking of conscious awareness
of emotion may powerfully serve the defences against experiencing
vulnerability and danger within the attachment relationship; if no
emotion is felt then one cannot be hurt by the other.

Characteristics of this constellation may be summarized as
follows.

Psychic murder syndrome

1. This is a complex mental organization and process in which
    emotional experience and relationships are continually "mur-
    dered"—an inner destruction which repeats an earlier one
    recurrently experienced with the care-giver. An original trauma
    is continually re-enacted, both internally and in relation to
    emotional partners. The "partner" (whether spouse/lover or
    therapist) is inevitably subjected to an experience of the original
    trauma (usually without being able to make much sense of
    what is happening). The purpose of this mental organization is,
    paradoxically, to protect against the danger of further violation
    of the core of the self and its true potential.
2. The pattern originates in an early environment that is
    experienced by the child as fundamentally hostile to his or
    her true self. The child's own initiatives and emotional
    communications are systematically rebuffed, mocked, ignored
    or actively punished. Instead are substituted the mother's
    desires to have a particular kind of child. The child registers
    this as a terrifying psychic murder (although such early
    perceptions cannot be elaborated in language). Profound
    distrust is established at the core of the child's being.
    Attachment relationships are felt to be essentially suffocating

because the original experience was that there was no psychic space for the child's true potential in the relationship with the mother. The mother's presence was experienced as simultaneously invasive/controlling and abandoning.

3.   A core of "paranoid" confusion develops, based on the child's perception that the one who is needed and is the source of comfort and nourishment is also the source of psychic murder. This state of confusion may be utterly intolerable. The child may split these perceptions, at times viewing the mother as loving, whilst at other times switching into the view of her as malevolent (this splitting is based upon the intolerable perception of actual qualities of the mother rather than the child's difficulty in integrating his/her own conflicting feelings of love and hate, as outlined in Kleinian theory).

4.   The child comes to feel that expression of emotional need and vulnerability is dangerous. Attachment associated with vulnerability is forbidden. In order to suppress this, the child identifies with the psychically murdering environment (a form of "identification with the aggressor"). The original psychic murder perpetrated by the environment is now continually repeated actively within the psyche. Emotions and emotional meaning are continually "strangled at birth". [This is somewhat similar to Bion's (1959) description of the internalization of a communication-mangling mother who engages in "attacks on linking".] The person's experience of emotions will contain blank areas; to some extent, normal emotions may be experienced in relation to others with whom he or she is *not* in an attachment relationship.

5.   Anxiety may be felt when emotion threatens to emerge into awareness. There may also be significant tendencies to somatize emotion, giving rise to various forms of physical distress. This occurs because although emotion and associated anxiety are generated, with physiological concomitants, these are denied access to consciousness and are thereby prevented from being processed through the mind. Anxiety and somatization may often be the predominant mode of expression of emotion.

6.   Because the child's true initiatives and emotions undergo continual annihilation, there is no basis for a true sense of identity. Instead there is an elaborate and continual adaptation

to the perceived requirements of others. This will not be apparent to the external observer who will mistakenly perceive each presentation as "real". (This is similar to accounts of "false self" and "as if" personality.)

7. The basic view of attachment as suffocating may give rise, early in the child's development, to a dissociative structure of mind, in which a secret area of non-compliance is preserved.

8. An enforcing structure is developed within the mind, with the task of ensuring that true emotional attachment, vulnerability, and trust do not take place beyond a certain point. This structure, characterized by cruelty and sadism, may be represented in dreams by a threatening gang or a murderer of some kind. If the person does begin to develop attachment and trust beyond the permitted level the internal gang may become very threatening, bringing about a severance of the relationship.

9. The inner psychic murder may not initially be apparent externally—for example, to the partner in a relationship. It is the inner emotional connection that is killed off. Ultimately this also becomes manifest in the external relationship.

10. Sexual relationships may be permitted, provided that these do not develop into emotional intimacy beyond a certain point. Initially the "partner" may be perceived in terms of the split perception of "good" (derived from the original splitting of the perceptions of mother). Sooner or later there will be a switch to the opposite emotional valence and the partner will be viewed with intense suspicion. Some of the time there may be recurrences of the intolerable state of confusion, where the partner is perceived as simultaneously good and bad (but in a confusing rather than integrated way). The original inner model of relationships as suffocating will be activated. At this point there may be a search for an alternative relationship. Such a sequence may be one basis for a pattern of compulsive promiscuity.

11. Despite the continual inner psychic murder, there may persist a hope of a relationship in which the "true self" can be expressed and recognized. At a deep level, this desire will be very powerful. If a suitable potential partner is found, there may be an attempt to relate on a deeper level of intimacy. This

endeavour will be accompanied by a combination of intense hope and anxiety. Some intimacy and trust may be established, but at a certain point the "anti-trust" enforcement will kick in, creating a radical disruption of the relationship. There will then ensue vigorous attempts to sever the relationship and drive the partner away, at the same time as some struggles to maintain the relationship. This is a time of intense conflict and turmoil, both internally and in the external relationship.

12. The motives for driving the partner away are both to preserve the core of true self potential from violation, *and* to protect the partner from permanent psychic murder. The partner may be perceived as an innocent victim who has stumbled unknowingly into a dark area of hidden sado–masochism. This gives rise to intolerable feelings of guilt and anxiety.

13. One paradox is that the greater the sense of trust that is established in the relationship, the greater the sense of danger and inner pressure to murder the emotional attachment. Deep feelings of confusion, uncertainty and paranoia are stirred up. This can create the sense that the relationship that contains most "good" is also the most "bad"—the deeper the love and trust, the greater the fear and turmoil.

14. The experience of the partner (or the therapist if the context is psychotherapy/psychoanalysis) gives some clue to the internal processes of psychic murder. There will be moments, or even prolonged periods, of emotional contact and communication of emotional meaning—but these will be abruptly and unexpectedly terminated, creating feelings in the partner of traumatic confusion, disappointment, and betrayal. Attempts to communicate emotionally will be met with a bewildering blankness (like an utter failure of the communicative aspects of projective identification).

15. Most of these processes take place unconsciously, but the person will often be aware of some aspects without being able to grasp the whole.

Characteristics of psychic murder syndrome

● An uncertain sense of identity. The person may adapt their presentation fluidly according to the perceived requirements of the context. He or she will often feel in some way inauthentic.

- A subtle sense of being somehow different from others (sometimes giving rise to fantasies of being an alien, for example). This may also be associated with feeling never genuinely known or understood by others.
- An altered experience of emotion. At times the person may not feel emotions and may be in a numbed or detached state of mind. This may not be particularly unpleasant since there is an absence of emotional pain. At other times, there may be fleeting experiences of emotion before they are suppressed. Varying patterns of partial experiencing and partial suppressing of emotions may develop. Anxiety may be felt as emotion threatens to emerge into awareness.
- Anxiety and somatization may often be the predominant forms of emotional expression.
- Attachment relationships are experienced as potentially suffocating.
- Dissociative states of mind and behaviour, involving promiscuity or other activities not "permitted" within the main attachment relationship. These represent the fundamental rebellion against the perceived suffocating qualities of the attachment relationship.
- Emotional or sexual promiscuity may occur.
- An internal prohibition against emotional attachment relationships involving vulnerability. This may be associated with an internal organization that becomes vigorously, and even violently, activated if vulnerability is developed beyond a permitted point.
- Intense conflict between a wish for authentic emotional contact and the belief that such contact, in the context of an attachment relationship, is fundamentally dangerous.
- Emotional relationships are repeatedly killed off. This psychic murder begins internally, but eventually becomes manifest in the external relationship. The partner's experience will be of hope and emotional connection being established, only to be followed repeatedly by a traumatic and confusing destruction of affective contact. This may occur not only in core attachment relationships, but also in other "friendships".

Some related theories—Kalsched, Rosenfeld, Winnicott, Bion

Kalsched's "self-care system and the psyche's auto-immune reaction"

Donald Kalsched, a Jungian analyst, has described a similar destructive organization derived from childhood trauma and abuse. He sees this as like a kind of psychic autoimmune disease in which the protective system attacks the person's own emotional vulnerability and feelings of shame. The abused child's aggression cannot be expressed towards the abuser if he or she is a primary care-giver, and so it is directed towards the child's own vulnerability and emotional need. Kalsched describes a dream dreamt by a patient immediately after she had for the first time allowed herself to feel vulnerable in response to the analyst's departure for a summer vacation. The night before the dream she had written a long letter to the analyst saying she must break off her therapy because she was becoming "too dependent". The dream was as follows:

> I am in my room, in bed. I suddenly realise I have forgotten to lock the doors to my apartment. I hear someone come into the building downstairs, walk to my apartment door—then walk in. I hear the footsteps approach the door of my room ... then open it. A very tall man with a white ghost-like face and black holes for eyes walks in with an axe. He raises it over my head and brings it down! ... I wake in terror. [Kalsched, 1996, p. 15]

In reality the patient usually double-locked the door to her bedroom and also carefully checked the outer door to the apartment. Kalsched comments:

> In the dream, the ghost-like man apparently has access to both doors, just as her father had had unrestricted access to the bedroom where she slept and also to her body. Often my patient—when only 8 years old—had heard his footsteps approach her room before his regular sexual violations of her. [p. 15]

Kalsched hypothesizes that the patient's admission of feelings of dependence and vulnerability in the previous session had been experienced as a dire threat of re-experiencing intolerable mental pain—the pain of need in relation to a care-giver, who might reject the need and instead impose abuse. The self-care system, based on identification with the aggressor (abuser) then came into play to sever her experience of vulnerability and need—and also to "split off" (with the axe) the memories of abuse, located in bodily experience, thereby preventing these entering the mind.

Kalsched summarizes the function of the self-care system as follows:

> Like the immune system of the body, the self-care system carries out its functions by actively attacking what it takes to be "foreign" or "dangerous" elements. Vulnerable parts of the self's experience in reality are seen as just such "dangerous" elements and are attacked accordingly. These attacks serve to undermine the hope in real object-relations and to drive the patient more deeply into fantasy. And just as the immune system can be tricked into attacking the very life it is trying to protect (auto-immune disease), so the self-care system can turn into a "self-destruct system" which turns the inner world into a nightmare of persecution and self-attack. [Kalsched, 1996, p. 24]

Rosenfeld's account of destructive narcissism and internal mafias

The Kleinian analyst, Herbert Rosenfeld (1971) described destructive organizations within the mind that are opposed to dependent relationships with others. He linked these to the operation of envy, as a manifestation of the death instinct. Driven by envy, the narcissistic character wishes to deny need and dependence:

> In terms of the infantile situation, the narcissistic patient wants to believe that he has given life to himself and is able to feed and look after himself. When he is faced with the reality of being dependent on the analyst, standing for the parents, particularly the mother, he would prefer to die, to be non-existent, to deny the fact of his birth, and also to destroy his analytic progress and insight regarding the child in himself, which he feels the analyst, representing the parents, has created. Frequently at this point the patient wants to give up the analysis but more often he acts out in a self-destructive way by spoiling his professional success and his personal relations. [p. 247]

Rosenfeld gives the example of a patient who dreamt of a small boy in a comatose condition; the patient stood nearby but did nothing to help and felt contemptuous of the doctor treating the boy. The dying boy clearly represented the patient's dependent self, which the patient prevented from gaining help. Any progress in the analysis tended to be countered by an upsurge of scornful and belittling thoughts about the analyst and an emotional withdrawal.

Rosenfeld described the existence of gang-like organizations within the mind of the narcissistic patient:

> The destructive narcissism of these patients appears often highly organised, as if one were dealing with a powerful gang dominated by a leader, who controls all the members of the gang to see that they support one another in making the criminal destructive work more effective and powerful. However, the narcissistic organisation not only increases the strength of the destructive narcissism, but it has a defensive purpose to keep itself in power and so to maintain the status quo. The main aim seems to be to prevent the weakening of the organisation and to control the members of the gang so that they will not desert the destructive organisation and join the positive parts of the self or betray the secrets of the gang to the police, the protecting superego, standing for the helpful analyst, who might be able to save the patient. Frequently when a patient of this kind makes progress in the analysis and wants to change he dreams of being attacked by members of the Mafia or adolescent delinquents and a negative therapeutic reaction sets in. This narcissistic organisation ... seems to have the purpose of maintaining the idealisation and superior powers of the destructive narcissism. To change, to receive help, implies weakness and is experienced as wrong or as a failure by the destructive narcissistic organisation which provides the patient with his sense of superiority." [p. 249]

Rosenfeld does not locate the origins of this narcissistic constellation in any traumatic or damaging childhood experience, other than that created by the patient's own innate feeling of envy which are hostile to the feeding mother. Thus, Rosenfeld sees the murderous hostility as residing within the infant, deriving from the envy component of the death instinct. It is not difficult to see in Rosenfeld's account a role of shame and humiliation. As he puts it, "to receive help implies weakness". Within his system, the narcissist aims to avoid the humiliation of displaying need or vulnerability.

James Grotstein (2000) has suggested that the internal gangs described by Rosenfeld might often originate when the child has dissociated from a dysfunctional family, substituting instead an imagined internal "little family", of which he or she is the head.

Winnicott's "false self"

The theory of the "false self"—based on excessive compliance with the mother's wishes and expectations—developed by the psycho-analyst and paediatrician, Donald Winnicott, is well-known. It is worth examining his account in some detail to see the similarities and differences with the theory of psychic murder syndrome.

Winnicott (1960) described a range of forms of false self, differing in degrees of severity:

> At one extreme: the False Self sets up as real and it is this that observers tend to think is the real person. In living relationships, work relationships, and friendships, however, the False Self begins to fail. In situations in which what is expected is a whole person, the False Self has some essential lacking. At this extreme the True Self is hidden. [pp. 142–143]

There are various lesser degrees of False Self which are more in the direction of health and normality. These allow the True Self to remain as a potential, protected by the False Self.

Winnicott believed the False Self develops in the early infant–mother relationship. Countering some of the excessively intra-psychic focus of certain psychoanalytic theorizing of the time, he emphasized the absolute dependence of the infant on the care-giving environment:

> To get to a statement of the relevant developmental processes it is essential to take into account the mother's behaviour and attitude, because in this field dependence is real, and near absolute. *It is not possible to state what takes place by reference to the infant alone.* [p. 144–145 italics in the original]

Winnicott saw the True Self as depending upon the mother's capacity to meet the infant's "spontaneous gesture or sensory hallucination", the result of this being that the child is able to use a symbol:

> ... the mother's adaptation is *good enough* and in consequence the infant begins to believe in external reality which appears and behaves as by magic (because of the mother's relatively successful adaptation to the infant's gestures and needs), and which acts in a way that does not clash with the infant's omnipotence. On this basis

the infant can gradually abrogate omnipotence. The True Self has a spontaneity, and this has been joined up with the world's events. The infant can now begin to enjoy the *illusion* of omnipotent creating and controlling, and then can gradually come to recognise the illusory element, the fact of playing and imagining. Here is the basis for the symbol which at first is both the infant's spontaneity or hallucination, *and also* the external object created and ultimately cathected. [p. 146]

Thus, according to Winnicott's account, the mother supports the infant's illusion of being the agent at the centre of his or her world. Because of this support, the infant can gradually distinguish illusion from reality and can develop an area of play and imagination. By contrast, the mother whose adaptation is not "good enough" requires too much adaptation and compliance from the infant. This excessive compliance is the False Self—an important function of which is to hide the True Self. Winnicott describes extreme cases where compliance is so pronounced that spontaneity is absent:

In the extreme examples of False Self development, the True Self is so well hidden that spontaneity is not a feature in the infant's living experiences. Compliance is then the main feature, with imitation as a speciality. [p. 147]

A very crucial point in Winnicott's thinking here is that the False Self is a defence—"a defence against that which is unthinkable, the exploitation of the True Self, which would result in its annihilation" (p. 147). The False Self manages to hide the vulnerable True Self—the core that must be protected at all costs. Violation of the core would be feared as a rape and pillage of one's soul. Winnicott described, in brackets, one kind of circumstance in which the True Self can be violated:

(If the True Self ever gets exploited and annihilated this belongs to the life of an infant whose mother was not only "not good enough" ... but was good and bad in a tantalisingly irregular manner. The mother here has as part of her illness a need to cause and to maintain a muddle in those who are in contact with her. This may appear in a transference situation in which the patient tries to make the analyst mad ... There may be a degree of this which can destroy the last vestiges of an infant's capacity to defend the True Self). [p. 147]

In this passage Winnicott hints at a more active—perhaps malevolent—hostility on the part of the mother towards the child's True Self. This may be closer to the idea of psychic murder syndrome. However, mostly Winnicott seems to be describing maternal incompetence in responding to the child's initiative rather than active hostility towards the True Self. This failure of the infant–mother relationship would lie in the realm of shame—the child's experience of not receiving the empathic understanding and recognition that is required. Winnicott's account does not describe the active internal destruction of emotion and relationship, in identification with that originally experienced from the mother, which is found in psychic murder syndrome.

Bion's theory of "attacks on linking"

W. R. Bion, a psychoanalyst within the Kleinian tradition, who made significant developments in the understanding of schizophrenic thought and the psychotic parts of the mind, described processes whereby certain patients "attack" the links between elements of the mind, such as thoughts, emotions, perceptions, and memories. The result is a destruction of meaning and of the capacity for normal thought.

Bion's clinical illustrations are not easy to summarize. He describes a patient who at times would develop a pronounced stutter that would have the effect of scattering his few words over a period of as much as a minute and a half; at one point the patient spoke of a difficulty in falling asleep and then remarked that he could not think because he was "wet". Bion interpreted as follows:

> From what I knew of this patient, I felt that ... somehow the wetness referred to an expression of hatred and envy such as he associated with urinary attacks on an object. I therefore said that ... he was afraid of sleep because for him it was the same thing as the oozing away of his mind itself. Further associations showed that he felt that good interpretations from me were so consistently and minutely split up by him that they became mental urine which then seeped uncontrollably away. Sleep was therefore inseparable from unconsciousness, which was itself identical with a state of mind-lessness which could not be repaired. He said "I am dry now".
> [Bion, 1959, p. 95]

Some readers might find Bion's example somewhat obscure. However, since he first formulated the idea, many analysts recognize some quite common phenomena as being related forms of "attacks on linking". Thus some patients may talk endlessly, but in such a way that it is extremely difficult for the analyst to grasp any underlying links between the diverse topics of the narrative. Meaning does not gradually emerge and organize around themes and anxieties, in the way that it does with other patients. There may be a kind of scattering of meaning, so that the analyst's experience is of having to gather together the scraps of dispersed emotional communication and piece them together like fragments of code. The emotional link between patient and analyst may similarly be severed, so that the patient acts as if there is no link.

According to Bion (1959), following the proposals of Melanie Klein (1957), these destructive attacks are driven by the patient's (and baby's) inherent hatred and envy of the feeding breast—"the inborn characteristics . . . producing attacks by the infant on all that links him to the breast, namely, primary aggression and envy" (p. 104). However, in addition, the mother may contribute to this by failing adequately to receive and process the infant's anxiety. Bion saw these psychotic processes as originating in the infant's relationship to the "part-object", the mother's breast. One of Bion's conceptual innovations at the time was to emphasize the emotional *functions* of the breast. He wrote:

> The conception of the part-object as analogous to an anatomical structure, encouraged by the patient's employment of concrete images as units of thought, is misleading because the part-object relationship is not with the anatomical structures only but with function, not with anatomy but with physiology, not with the breast but with feeding, poisoning, loving, hating. [p. 102]

Bion suggested that one of the important functions of the mother is to be receptive to the child's communication of anxiety and to transform this by her empathy and thought, so that her responses to the child are soothing. According to Bion, the child's transmission of anxiety is by projective identification—a process that Klein described as a phantasy of locating part of the self in the object, but which Bion elaborated as an actual communication (the precise mechanism of which is unspecified). When this communicative process between infant and mother proceeds well, the baby is soothed and his or her mental development is facilitated. He reconstructed the early development of the patient in his example as follows:

> My deduction was that in order to understand what the child wanted the mother should have treated the infant's cry as more than a demand for her presence. From the infant's point of view she should have taken into her, and thus experienced, the fear that the child was dying. It was this fear that the child could not contain. He strove to split it off together with the part of the personality in which it lay and project it into the mother. An understanding mother is able to experience the feeling of dread, that this baby was striving to deal with by projective identification, and yet retain a balanced outlook. This patient had to deal with a mother who could not tolerate experiencing such feelings and reacted either by denying them ingress, or alternatively by becoming a prey to the anxiety which resulted from introjection of the infant's feelings. [p. 104]

In this passage, Bion is describing a mother who could not tolerate knowing the baby's anxiety and who therefore rejected his communication. In this way the mother engaged in an "attack on linking", giving rise to an internal mother that continued to do this. However, Bion emphasized that the problem arises from a combination of internal and external factors. The lack of receptivity of a mother contributes to the formation of an internal mother hostile to emotional communication, but the malignant development is also driven by the infant's own envy and hatred. Bion explains his view as follows:

> The seriousness of these attacks is enhanced if the mother displays the kind of unreceptiveness which I have described, and is diminished, but not abolished, if the mother can introject the infant's feelings and remain balanced; the seriousness remains because the psychotic infant is overwhelmed with hatred and envy of the mother's ability to retain a comfortable state of mind although experiencing the infant's feelings. This was clearly brought out by a patient who insisted that I must go through it with him, but was filled with hate when he felt that I was able to do so without a breakdown. Here we have another aspect of destructive attacks upon the link, the link being the capacity of the analyst to introject the patient's projective identifications. Attacks on the link, therefore,

are synonymous with attacks on the analyst's, and originally the mother's, peace of mind. The capacity to introject is transformed by the patient's envy and hate into greed devouring the patient's psyche; similarly, peace of mind becomes hostile indifference. [pp. 105–106]

Thus, in his account of the development of "attacks on linking", Bion describes the role of a mother who is unreceptive to the child's emotional communications—rather like Winnicott's description of the mother who fails to respond to the child's True Self. The attack on emotional meaning continues within the child's own mind, in identification with the communication-rejecting mother. However, Bion sees the process as driven, or at least greatly exacerbated, by the infant's envious attacks on the mother's function, which transform his or her perception of her intention and activity. Through the operation of envy, a "good" mother can be transformed in the child's perception into a "bad" mother. This emphasis upon the contribution of the child's innate envy and hatred, and their interplay with the actual characteristics of the parents, is a recurrent feature of the Kleinian tradition within psychoanalysis.

However, I have noticed that often patients who appear very attacking of the analyst's attempted communications will cease to be so when they feel that their experience and anxiety are properly understood. What may fuel attacks which appear full of hatred and envy is a perception that the analyst is convinced of the correctness of his or her view. At such times, the analyst is perceived as serenely secure in a belief in his or her intellectual, emotional and moral truth—and as unreceptive to the patient's communications of anguish. This tends to repeat a childhood perception of the mother as walled off from the child's distress and as self-righteous in her view of herself and of her maternal functions. The "cure" for the patient's (and child's) hostile state of mind is an empathic response from the analyst (or mother) that expresses a recognition and understanding of the distress, including particularly the analyst's (or mother's) contribution to that distress. This indicates how the distress is closely related to shame, the cure for which is also an empathic response. A further related point is that if a patient is frequently in states of great agitation and confusion, then it is quite to be expected that he or she might feel some envy, alongside gratitude, if the analyst appears always calm, thoughtful, and able to make sense of the patient's turbulent mind. Acknowledging this does not imply that the patient has an unusual level of constitutional envy, but simply recognizes that those who are in a state of anguish and despair may envy those who appear to have peace of mind. This envy can be diminished to the extent that the patient can recognize that the analyst is struggling and, to some extent, *suffering* with them in the exploration of their anguish.

Comparisons with psychic murder syndrome

The theories of Kalsched, Rosenfeld, Winnicott, and Bion all have some similarities with the formulation of psychic murder syndrome. Kalsched's is perhaps closest, in his account of the child's identification with the hostile or abusive care-giver, such that the "self-care system" turns against his or her own vulnerability; in this way the abuse is continued internally. Rosenfeld also describes internal attacks on the person's feelings of dependence and vulnerability—but attributes these to the aggressive (envious) aspects of narcissism, which aim to deny dependence or need and to sustain illusions of being self-created and self-sufficient. The early role of the environment is not considered. Bion describes attacks on emotional meaning and the infantile link to the breast, which, like Rosenfeld, he attributes to the workings of envy. However, in addition, Bion considers the contribution of the mother in her lack of receptivity to the child's communications of anguish. Winnicott gives an account of False Self development and a suppression of the True Self, deriving from a failure on the part of the mother to respond creatively to the child's own gesture or initiative. According to Winnicott, the "good enough" mother supports the child's illusions of omnipotence until the child is ready to surrender these in the face of reality—and thus, by implication, the mother protects the child from *too early* and *too much* awareness of dependence, so that envy is not unduly provoked. The mother who fosters a compliant False Self development requires an excessive adaptation by the child to *her* initiatives.

The formulation of psychic murder syndrome is in some ways close to Winnicott's theory of the False Self, but in addition indicates how the attempted "murder" of the True Self is continued internally, and how the attacks on emotional relationships are perpetrated compulsively and unconsciously. Such development does not require overt abuse (although this may occur), but is based on the child's perception that his or her authentic self is not recognized or accepted, and that, instead, an alternative version is required by the mother. An important feature of this process is that the mother is perceived as *hostile* to the authentic self, and as invasive and controlling—threatening the core of the self. The damaging effect is probably greatest if the father is either absent, or collusive with the mother's stance, or is himself abusive and rejecting. Through this experience, a profound distrust of attachment relationships is established. This does not mean that attachment is then avoided completely, but that the person's later attachment relationships will be pervaded by intense conflict and anxiety—and that the anxiety will motivate repeated attacks on the relationship and upon the sense of emotional vulnerability. The process is not seen as driven by the child's envy, as portrayed in the theories of Rosenfeld and Bion—but if such a factor were in operation, it would no doubt compound the difficulty of the situation considerably.

Toxic shame associated with sexual abuse

A teenage girl, who ran away from home to London, suffered a terrifying gang rape when lured to a flat where she had been expecting to receive care and protection after being "befriended" by a man she had met in the street. The gang, which included two women, imposed a variety of sexual humiliations and physical injuries, whilst taunting her verbally. Her immediate reaction was to dissociate, feeling that she was not really present and that it was not really happening. This dissociation made her all the more helpless and passive in her response to the situation. Afterwards, she became very disturbed, developing chronic symptoms of post-traumatic stress, with severe anxiety, panic, intrusive flashback images, and a pervasive distrust of others. When she was seen in psychotherapy some years later, one of the most difficult problems to address was her strongly established belief that she was "a slag" who had been asking to be raped. Basically she believed that the rape was her fault. Associated with this belief was overwhelming shame, such that she viewed herself as not fit to live—and did indeed engage in frequent acts of self-harm which were at times life-threatening.

It is not easy to convey the depth and intensity of such toxic shame—for it is of a quality that is a quantum leap from the distressing feelings of chagrin, embarrassment, and disappointment in the self, that most of us are prone to experience from time to time. This shame is lethal—it poisons the soul and completely corrodes any vestiges of self-esteem. No pride or pleasure in the self can survive its onslaught. It may be related to what Fonagy *et al.* (2002) refer to as "ego-destructive shame". They see this as arising when a child is subject to very severe interpersonal trauma and abuse that cannot be processed and alleviated via the capacity for mentalization. The latter is "the process by which we realise that having a mind mediates our experience of the world" (p. 3) and "involves both a self-reflective and an interpersonal component ... [which] ... provide the child with a capacity to distinguish inner from outer reality, intrapersonal mental and emotional processes from inter-personal communications" (p. 4). This mentalization capacity is thought to derive in part from the mother's relating to the child as a person with a mind. However, in the case of the child's experience of a mother who appears hostile, the child may be inhibited from developing mentalization because a perception of the mother's mind may be too threatening. Without the capacity for mentalization, shame is experienced and experienced in a much more concrete and absolute way. It is as if the normal experience in shame, of wanting to disappear, is experienced as a compelling and concrete annihilation of the self. Fonagy *et al.* (2002) comment:

> ... brutalisation in the context of attachment relationships generates intense shame. This, if coupled with a history of neglect and a consequent weakness in mentalisation, becomes a likely trigger for violence against the self or others, because of the intensity of the humiliation experiences when the trauma cannot be processed and attenuated via mentalisation. Unmentalised shame, which remains unmediated by any sense of distance between feelings and objective realities, is then experienced as the destruction of the self. We have called it "ego-destructive shame" [pp. 12–13]

In the case of the woman who was raped by a gang, she took into herself the mockery and insults—particularly the accusation of being a "slag"—and then for years continually replayed the accusation internally. This and other terms of abuse would be endlessly recycled by inner hallucinatory voices until she would relieve the tension by some act of self-harm. She recalled that it had been particularly the two women in the gang who had taunted her with such insults. It seemed likely therefore that the women had been engaged in an act of projective identification, or "imposed identity" (Mollon, 2001a, 2002), whereby unwanted aspects of their own self-image were forcibly evoked in the victim. She was then left in a state of having been invaded, or colonized, by an "alien self" (Fonagy et al., 2002).

Whilst severe and sadistic interpersonal trauma during adult life can engender a deeply disturbed and altered state of mind, which can be persistent, more commonly the psychiatric clinician encounters the damage caused by recurrent abuse in childhood. Many of the patients with various forms of "borderline personality disorder", who suffer disabling anxiety, mood swings, unstable relationships, and tendencies to self-harm, report childhood backgrounds involving physical, sexual and emotional abuse within highly disturbed families (Allen, 2001; Mollon, 1996, 2002). In such instances, the damage is not simply due to the fact of suffering abuse, but it is also crucially to do with the meaning of this occurring at the hands of those to whom the child would naturally turn to for nurturance and protection. Fonagy et al. (2002) argue as follows:

> Why should the brutalisation of affectional bonds, whether in the context of relationships with parents or with intimate peers, be associated with such an intense and destructive sense of self-disgust verging on self-hatred? Once again, there is a paradox: the shame concerns being treated as a physical object in the very context where special personal recognition is expected. Overwhelming mental pain is associated with experiencing a discrepancy between the representation of an actual self, based on how one is being treated, and the representation of the ideal shape of the self (Joffe & Sandler, 1967). The expectation of being seen and understood as a feeling and thinking person, which is created by the attachment context, clashes violently with the brutalised person's objectification and dehumanisation. Shame is a higher order derivative of this basic affect of pain. Unbearable shame is generated through the incongruity of having one's humanity negated, exactly when one is legitimately expecting to be cherished. [p. 426]

In this way, Fonagy and his colleagues manage to link the early idea of shame as arising from *intrapsychic* discrepancy between the actual self and ideal self, proposed by Piers and Singer (1953), with the shame arising from the *interpersonal experience* of abuse by care-givers within an attachment relationship.

A further aspect of the shame arising from interpersonal trauma and abuse is the intensely negative view of self that may be maintained in order to preserve a good image of the abusive parent. Fairbairn (1952) called this the "moral defence". Shengold (1989) described something similar in his discussion of "soul murder". He explains a subtle aspect of this—that the abused child may find it more tolerable to preserve a delusional view of the self as "bad" and the care-giver as "good" than to suffer the "annihilation of identity, of the feeling of the self" that would follow from perceiving the care-giver accurately and experiencing the "terrifying intensity of fear and rage" (p. 26). Thus it is better to view the self as bad than to have the self annihilated. Such reversals of responsibility can be very entrenched and quite extreme. For example, one patient, who had been extensively sexually abused by her father over many years, refused to accept the term "abuse", arguing that she had permitted the sexual activity. When asked at what age her father first abused her, she carefully rephrased the question and replied "I first allowed my father to touch me sexually was when I was age three".

There are many aspects of the sense of self that are damaged by interpersonal abuse within an attachment relationship (Mollon, 1993, 1996, 2001). In particular, the sense of agency or efficacy (Slavin & Pollock, 1997), including the sense of being able to evoke an appropriate and empathic emotional response in the other, may be severely impaired. The result is what Kohut (1972) called "narcissistic rage"—an overwhelming shame-fuelled storm of unmanageable affect that smashes like a tidal wave onto the fragile functioning of the abused person's ego. This state of being flooded by shame and rage may bring about further shame.

Summary

A complex personality organization may be discerned in some patients who have experienced their childhood relationship with their mother as consistently opposed to their own authentic initiatives. As a result of this perception of maternal hostility to their "true" self, there is a retreat from the normal wish to make emotional contact with others. The child becomes outwardly compliant, at least to some extent, whilst identifying with the psychically murderous environment, continually killing off potential emotional relationships. The internal psychic murder is endlessly repeated in order to prevent the danger of reaching out emotionally and vulnerably and again experiencing annihilation from the external other—better to take control of the killing off and repeat it actively and internally rather than suffer it passively from outside. Emotions are felt to be dangerous, because of their association with vulnerability, and are therefore continually blocked, becoming expressed instead somatically. Sexual relationships are experienced as invasive and abusive. The account of psychic murder syndrome may be compared with some other similar psychoanalytic descriptions—Rosenfeld's "internal mafia", Bion's "attacks on linking", Kalsched's "self-care system", and Winnicott's "false self". None of these other formulations capture the idea of the child's (unconscious) perception of the mother's profound hostility to his or her true self.

The childhood background of patients suffering from psychic murder syndrome would probably not appear grossly abusive. Such trauma may be quite subtle. However, where there has been severe interpersonal trauma and abuse, perhaps including sexual abuse, the child may grow up to be an adult imbued with *toxic shame*. This is overwhelming, sweeping all self-esteem away. It may be related to what Fonagy and colleagues call "ego destructive shame" and Shengold calls "soul murder". Sometimes it may be lethal. The person who has been extensively abused as a child may live continually on the edge of a precipice—ever in danger of being tripped, by the inevitable "slings and arrows" of everyday life, into an inferno of narcissistic rage and toxic shame.

CHAPTER FOUR

Jealousy

"Jealousy is one of those affective states, like grief, that may be regarded as normal. If anyone appears to be without it, the inference is justified that it has undergone severe repression and consequently plays all the greater part in his unconscious mental life"

Freud, 1922, p. 223

"A person who suffers an instinctual frustration experiences intense unpleasure, and we take it as a matter of course that he should feel hatred against the frustrating object. Nor does it seem to us a problem that he should feel envy toward another person who is more gratified than he—that is, that he should identify that person with himself and experience the more bitterly the contrast between this empathy of his imagination and the unpleasant reality and, out of this contrast, should develop aggressive tendencies against the luckier one. Jealousy is obviously a combination of this envy with that hatred ..."

Fenichel, 1935, p. 349

J ealousy erupts violently, often without warning, brutally trampling on feelings of love and trust. The effect can be traumatizing for both the one who feels it and the one to whom it is directed. Its torment is intense and insistent, accompanied by powerful physiological concomitants, the whole body shaking and pulsating with shock. Some people rarely experience the turmoil of jealousy—instead they create it in others (White, 1980; White & Mullen, 1989). These are the *agents* of jealousy, the ones who always turn away first, and who thereby force their partner to suffer (projectively) what they repudiate from their own experience.

Jealousy is such a ubiquitous and intense emotion that we might wonder what function it serves. It does not make for happiness. Indeed it can often be so disruptive to a relationship that it brings about the very abandonment or betrayal that is feared. Jealousy is often regarded as fundamentally destructive. Popular self-help and inspirational literature urges sufferers to strive to overcome their possessiveness and to attend to their own underlying feelings of insecurity (Ellis, 1998; Lobsenz, 1975; Schoenfeld, 1979)—the implication being that a secure person with healthy self-esteem would not experience jealousy. Thus jealousy is regarded as a sign of weakness, of inappropriate possessiveness—and so the pain of jealousy is mixed also with shame. Shame and jealousy fuel each other: the perception of a rival contains the idea of one's own inadequacy compared to an other, and hence gives rise to shame and jealousy—which gives rise to further shame and feelings of inadequacy—in turn giving rise to further jealousy—and so on. The Oedipal situation—the childhood prototype of later jealousy— inevitably contains shame since the child is bound to feel inadequate in comparison to the adult rival. Naïve idealism may confound the shame of the jealous adult. Thus, the anthropologist Margaret Mead, in an early paper, written when she was aged about 30, denounced jealousy as "undesirable, a festering spot in every personality so afflicted, an ineffective negativistic attitude which is more likely to lose than to gain any goal" and speculated that it might be possible to eliminate or reduce jealousy by, for example, the Soviet experiments in socialism, or through living in a cosmopolitan city such as London or New York! (Clanton & Smith, 1998, p. 127). Even some recent commentators have suggested that jealousy is derived from capitalist society and culture (Bhugra, 1993)

—but Buss (2000) observes that "Cultures in tropical paradises that are entirely free of jealousy exist only in the romantic minds of optimistic anthropologists, and in fact have never been found" (p. 32). Neu (1980) comments:

> It was one of the hopes of the sixties (as of many other periods) that by restructuring social relations it might be possible to eliminate jealousy and other painful, "bourgeois", passions. This was the hope that inspired many in the commune movement. It has been largely, I think, a failed hope. Jealousy, envy and possessiveness reasserted themselves despite the best efforts to keep them down. [p. 427]

Violent feelings of jealousy, often hidden before erupting with cataclysmic force, may shatter both mind and body. Indeed many studies show that jealousy is a root cause of much violence and even murder against sexual partners (Buss, 2000). So what is jealousy for? Does it in fact have a useful function?

Evolutionary perspectives

> Nonjealous men and women, however, are not our ancestors, having been left in the evolutionary dust by rivals with different passionate sensibilities. We all come from a long lineage of ancestors who possessed the dangerous passion. [Buss, 2000, p. 5]

The recently emerged field of evolutionary (or Darwinian) psychology and psychiatry (e.g. Buss, 1999, 2000; Gilbert & Bailey, 2000; Stevens & Price, 2000; Thornhill & Palmer, 2000)[1] suggests some important functions of jealousy that are inevitable products of processes of natural selection for reproductive fitness. From this perspective, jealousy has evolved as a necessary safeguard to detect and defend against the threat of sexual deception and infidelity that threaten the propagation of the individual's genes. According to this evolutionary view, it is the *absence* of jealousy in a relationship that would be abnormal.

Whilst earlier psychoanalytic thinking did see psychopathology as rooted in evolutionary history—for example, Freud's theory of the primal hoard (1913, 1939)—such ideas were not grounded in a clear neo-Darwinian understanding of the primacy of the principle of reproductive success (as opposed to individual survival). Contemporary evolutionary perspectives—which are compatible with modern psychoanalytic frameworks based on attachment theory (Migone & Liotti, 1998; Liotti, 2000)—consider that "traits are selected not on the basis of arbitrary definitions of happiness, well-being or social conformity, but by their effects on reproduction rates in subsequent generations" (Gilbert, 1998, p. 354). Success in transmitting genes to the next generation, *rather than the survival (or well-being) of the individual*, is the guiding principle behind the evolutionary selection of behaviour (Barkow *et al.*, 1992; Hamilton, 1964)—but it is important to understand that this powerful motivation on behalf of the genes is to a large extent inaccessible to conscious awareness and is not *experienced* as a motivation. According to this principle, men and women will have evolved different attitudes towards mating, and different modes of sexual jealousy, as a result of the asymmetry of their positions in relation to propagation of their genes. Conflicting desires may be present which reflect the impact of older and newer reproductive strategies. For example, on the one hand, males will have evolved a desire to impregnate as many females as possible, in competition with other males, in order to maximize transmission of their genes; on the other hand, the development of large brained infants, whose "premature" birth means that much care has to be invested in them by the mother, has given rise to the reproductive value of stable and committed relationships. In the transition to *Homo sapiens* and the development of a hunter–gathering way of life, males were required by females for more than just their sperm. Females, therefore, in selecting a mate, seek evidence of the capacity for commitment and kindness, as well as indicators of status and health. There are inherent tensions in this evolutionary history. For example, within men there may be competing and contradictory inclinations towards promiscuous reproduction and the establishment of a stable family; in contemporary Western society, a common pattern is for the promiscuous reproductive strategy to be pursued first, followed later by the strategy based on a committed relationship. Glantz and Moehl (2000) comment as follows:

As men became more reliable mates and parents, they became more valuable resources for women. Consequently, there was pressure for women to compete for males and their resources. With the formation of a male–female bond, infidelity became a bigger issue, especially for the male who, more likely to invest in one female, deeply feared being cuckolded. Similarly, females deeply feared loss of emotional commitment of their mate to another, and males were thus required to exhibit commitment and put limits of their promiscuity. Pursuing additional mating opportunities would grievously offend his mate and might compromise the survival of their existing children. In this complex situation, the "best" reproductive strategy became unclear and elusive. ... It is in man's genetic interest to mate with many women, but doing so will not necessarily make him happy. Ever since hunter–gatherer times, men have also been endowed with a desire for a family, children and emotional bonds as well as for multiple mating opportunities. Consequently, in men, phylogenetically older and newer reproductive strategies are in eternal conflict. [pp. 181–188]

The reproductive strategies of men and women are both inter-dependent and *in conflict*. For example, since women may seek evidence of commitment before mating, some men may have evolved strategies of providing false cues to commitment. In turn, women may then have evolved increased abilities to detect deception:

As women developed the ability to detect deception, they imposed selection pressures on men to become better deceivers. And so the co-evolutionary spiral continues, with each increment in one sex producing reciprocal evolutionary change in the other. Adaptations in one sex lead to counter-adaptations in the other, and those in turn lead to further counter-adaptations and counter-counter-adaptations. As long as the strategies of the sexes are in some degree of conflict, this co-evolutionary spiral will continue unabated. At the current moment in time, we are poised in the middle of this spiral, with women being excellent detectors of deception, as indicated by their superiority over men in decoding nonverbal signals. Men, in turn, can be notoriously skilled at deceiving women. [Buss, 2000, pp. 44–45]

Gender differences in jealousy

Men may have evolved much stronger reactions of jealousy to the idea of the woman having sex with another man, as opposed to emotional infidelity, which may be more important to the woman.

This evolutionary difference between the sexes is because, prior to the availability of contraception, a female's infidelity could potentially have far more severe genetic consequences than the infidelity of the male. Whilst the female always "knows" that 50% of her offspring's genes are hers, the male can run the risk of caring for offspring that are not his own (i.e. do not carry his genes) if the female has been sexually unfaithful. There is no reciprocal reproductive risk to the female if the male is unfaithful; her reproduction and transmission of her own genes are not in any way compromised by the male's infidelity. What the female does have to lose is the resources and protection if the male abandons her for another—i.e. if the relationship and bonding is threatened. Thus, whilst there are painful costs of infidelity for both males and females, the genetic costs are quite different and much higher for males. Moreover, what complicates the relationship between the sexes even further is that there may be reproductive benefits to the female if she is secretly unfaithful; various factors, including phenomena called "sperm retention" and "sperm competition" (Birkhead & Moller, 1998) mean that, although retaining her mate is an important motivation, by being sexually unfaithful a woman can maximize her chances of her egg being fertilized by a sperm carrying superior genes. Buss (2000) refers to this as a "'mixed' mating strategy—ensuring devotion and investment from one man while acquiring good genes from another" (p. 162).[2] A study showed that women who are having affairs are more likely to engage in their illicit sexual liaisons when they were ovulating, whilst sex with their husbands was most likely to occur when they were not ovulating (Buss, 2000).[3] Thus, in terms of strategies of reproduction evolved prior to the development of contraception, it would appear that the women in the study would have sex with their illicit partner at a time when they were likely to conceive, whilst sex with their regular partner would seem to be in the service of retaining his loyalty rather than directed towards reproduction—reproductive strategies that would be essentially non-conscious, even though acting as a strong determinant of behaviour. Buss (2000) notes that although men are generally recognized to be more promiscuous than women and that this impression is supported by scientific studies, there is also evidence that female infidelity may also have been selected by evolution:

— problem of PC aspect, which is hard to an evolutionary explain, see also The Psychology of PC [?]

If ancestral women were naturally inclined to be flawlessly faithful, men would have had no evolutionary catalyst for jealousy. ... The intensity of men's jealousy provides a psychological clue that betrays women's desire for men other than their regular partners. [p. 17]

Whilst females may have evolved a tendency to be sexually unfaithful, males may have evolved strategies of preventing this. Thus, males are more prone to extremes of sexual guarding and sexual jealousy (Symonds, 1979; Wilson & Daly, 1992; Buss *et al.*, 1992; Buss, 2000). Gilbert *et al.* (2000) draw attention to the line in the Beatles song "Run for your life" (from the LP *Rubber Soul*), which vividly illustrates male jealousy with the stark words:

I'd rather see you dead little girl than to be with another man.

Empirical studies, using objective physiological measures as well as subjective reports, show that men produce stronger responses than women, of jealousy in general, and to sexual infidelity in particular, whilst women react more to emotional infidelity (Buss *et al.*, 1992; Buss, 2000). This finding holds across cultures (Buunk *et al.*, 1996) and is *not* accounted for by a belief that if a woman has sex she is likely also to be emotionally involved (Wiederman & Kendell, 1999). The caricature of the possessive and controlling male, jealously guarding his mate as if she were a part of his territory, and fiercely warding off other rival males, may represent a profoundly "politically incorrect" and pre-feminist mode of behaviour—but it may actually express the genetic programming evolved over many thousands of years. Buss (2000) comments:

Co-evolutionary logic tells us that men have evolved strategies to prevent reproductive losses by guarding their wives more diligently and punishing them for signs of straying through verbal abuse, emotional manipulation, jealous rages, beatings, and sometimes the threat of death. ... Women's infidelity, in turn, has become more cryptic, enigmatic, and deceptive over evolutionary time to evade these costs. [p. 176]

In coming into conflict with contemporary cultural values, which denigrate male attitudes of control and possession towards women, such evolved reproductive strategies can be a source of

O/D – include LINK however
this gay psychology.
∂ Shame –

84   SHAME AND JEALOUSY

shame for the man (Glantz & Moehl, 2000). The educated "New Man" may try to be non-possessive, enlightened and loving, relating to his female partner as a free individual entitled to her autonomy—but then may be shocked and ashamed when he finds to his dismay that an older phylogenetic programme is suddenly triggered, releasing violent physiological responses and seemingly the most unrefined of male behaviour. Bailey (1987) comments as follows on our embeddedness in early phylogenetic brain responses that can be a source of shame and guilt:

> We must acknowledge that our species possesses the neural hardware and many of the motivational–emotional proclivities ... of our reptilian ancestors, and, thus our drives, inner subjective feelings, fantasies and thoughts are thoroughly conditioned by emanations from the R-complex. The reptilian carry-overs provide the automatic, compulsive, urgency to much human behaviour, where free will steps aside and persons act as they have to act, often despising themselves in the process for their hatreds, prejudices, compulsions, conformity, deceptiveness and guile. [p. 63]

The male who experiences jealousy as a result of perceiving that his partner has been, or potentially may be, sexually unfaithful will suffer shame also as a direct result of his self-perception of failing in sexual competition and of falling in social ranking (Gilbert & McGuire, 1998). Shame is part of the constellation of submissive and subordinate behaviour, designed (by evolution) to be adaptive in avoiding injury from more dominant competitors. In today's society, the jealous male is caught in a pincer between phylogenetically older responses and the need to adapt to current cultural values—the combination of which may force him into a deepening spiral of shame that can be experienced as catastrophic. When he attempts to avoid the shame inherent in losing his mate to another male, he may fall back on older responses of fighting off the rival and trying to control the behaviour of the female; however, this then brings him crashing up against the shame of behaving in ways that are against current societal values. Thus he may, as if his life were an emotional pinball machine, bounce between these two sources of shame, along the way down smashing into other agonies of guilt, helplessness and despair—this whole constellation appearing quite unmanageable at times. I have heard such experiences described by

a number of male patients, who also report how the woman in the situation looks on with apparent bemusement and scorn at the intensity of the man's state of agitation; because their reproductive strategies and needs are different, albeit complementary, men and women have difficulty understanding some of each other's most primitive and compelling emotional responses.

The need to combine evolutionary and psychodynamic explanations

If the theory of evolution is taken seriously, as providing at least a partial explanation of human characteristics, then we must accept that non-consciously our behaviour and emotions are driven and organized by strategies to maximize the successful propagation of our genes.[4] These reproductive strategies will be at work in our attachment-seeking and mating behaviours, and in our care and nurture of our children. Mostly, these motivational forces are not available to introspection and direct awareness. Whilst evolutionary theory looks at the developmental history of the *species* as it has adapted to changing environments and to competing demands, psychoanalysis examines the development of the individual mind and the adaptations that have had to be made whilst growing up within the family of origin. Both perspectives are necessary for an understanding of the individual.

Psychoanalysis and evolutionary psychology are somewhat similar and overlapping frameworks. Both are developmental and biological theories, looking for an understanding of present behaviour in the light of earlier circumstances. Both see conflict, anxiety, and unhappiness as inherent in the human condition—and locate jealousy as an unavoidable feature of this. Similarly, both consider that human misery can be alleviated by understanding and accepting human nature. Both theories are wide-ranging and are open to criticisms that they are difficult to prove or disprove—and both tend to evoke strong emotional reactions.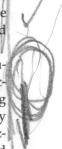

A further point of contact between psychoanalysis and evolutionary psychology is that both emphasize sexuality (i.e. reproduction) in one way or another as the ultimate motivation-directing behaviour. Whilst Freud's original emphasis directly upon sexuality —libido and Eros—was superseded in later psychoanalytic theorizing by a focus on the infant's seeking of relationship, nurture, and attachment with the care-giver; these aspects of motivation too can be seen as part of the broad evolved strategy of ensuring reproductive success. Indeed, contemporary psychoanalytic attachment theory, derived from Bowlby (who was himself a significant Darwin scholar—Bowlby, 1991) is highly compatible with evolutionary perspectives. Fonagy *et al.* (2002), commenting on the replacement of the earlier notion of "survival of the fittest" with the theory of "inclusive fitness" (Wenegrat, 1990)—in which the survival of close relatives sharing common genes may be favoured as much as that of the individual—see attachment as crucial to this:

> The concept of "inclusive fitness" places attachment theory at the center stage of evolutionary socio-biology as a key behavioral mechanism mediating the establishment of genetic proximity, for attachment is the process that ensures that we know whose survival will advantage the reproduction of our genes. [p. 122]

Moreover, they see attachment as serving multiple evolutionary functions—for example: the facilitation of the care of children; a marker of those with whom one should *not* mate because of the biological risks associated with incest; a marker for reciprocal altruism.

Whilst evolutionary theory can offer insights into the deep (distal) motivations that structure human behaviour to ensure reproduction of genes—motivations which are inaccessible to conscious awareness and introspection—psychoanalysis describes, and makes accessible to conscious awareness, the (proximal) emotions, impulses, conflicts, and anxieties that have arisen through evolutionary selection, and which human beings struggle to regulate and integrate in their daily lives and relationships. It is within the realm of psychoanalysis that we can locate the early roots of jealousy in the Oedipus complex, in envious and greedy wishes towards the mother, and in rivalry with siblings, and where we can also discern the contribution of mechanisms of defence, such as projection, which act to enhance jealousy, or such as denial or disavowal, which act to block perceptions that would otherwise give rise to jealousy. Undoubtedly, more work needs to be done on the interface between evolutionary theory and psychoanalysis. Of crucial significance here is that both perspectives see jealousy as inherent human tendencies.

→ how all this affects
gay males & females —
gay is crucial
how (the) gays perceive
women
JEALOUSY   87

A jealous woman

Some women become alarmed if the man shows any sexual interest, even if of only the most rudimentary nature, in another woman. For example, one violently jealous patient would covertly check her partner's pulse rate as they watched television together. If she felt that his pulse rate was increasing when an attractive woman appeared on the screen, she would smack him around the face. Similarly, if she noticed that he looked at a woman in the street, she would berate him fiercely. Usually her man would appear genuinely bemused at her accusations, protesting that he was not aware of having looked or felt any sexual interest in another woman. As we explored the meaning of her reactions, she disclosed her belief that if her partner loved her he would not show any interest at all in other women. Therefore she felt that if he looked at a woman in the street or on television this must mean that he did not love her and might therefore leave her—and moreover, she felt it meant she was defective in some way. This patient experienced some relief when the evolutionary perspective was explained to her. It was pointed out that the male brain has probably been selected through evolution in terms of a continuous scanning for attractive women, whereas the female brain may not have developed this characteristic to the same extent. This made sense to her and she had not thought about her husband's behaviour in this way before. She remarked (referring to her partner's looking at women in the street) "Oh you mean its like a reflex—like he can't help it—he doesn't even know he is doing it—that's what he says—he is not aware of looking". She began to see that her partner's looking at other women did not mean that he was going to leave her—and, in fact, he did appear to be extremely devoted to her.

Whilst part of this patient's jealousy responded to a biological explanation, another aspect required a psychodynamic interpretation. In the past she had been extremely promiscuous, using her capacity to attract men as a source of self-esteem and feelings of power. She still resorted to sex addictively as a means of soothing and restoring a sense of well-being. Fortunately her partner was usually able and willing to oblige her desire for sex several times a day. However, with some exploration, she was eventually able to acknowledge that she still experienced at times the old urges to pick up men promiscuously whenever her mood and self-esteem became at all dysphoric. It was possible to put to her the hypothesis that she was projectively attributing to her partner her own impulses to be promiscuous which she was attempting to deny within herself. She could then see that her suspiciousness of her partner, such that she would quiz him about women that he might have seen during his day at work, was really an expression of her own repudiated wishes to be unfaithful. As a result of this insight she became aware of her conflict between her impulses to resort to her old methods of restoring self-esteem through promiscuity and her feeling now that this was incompatible with her love for her partner. However, it was possible to clarify that her impulses to restore her self-esteem through promiscuous sex did not imply any lack of love for her partner since such sexual encounters were always utterly depersonalized. Another crucial point was that she did not herself experience sexual desire for other men—what she desired was to be the object of *their* desire and in that way to experience sexual power—an essentially narcissistic exercise. If she focused on another man it was in order to seduce him—not because she desired him. Therefore, if she noticed her partner's eyes straying towards another woman she would conclude that he was operating on the same basis of planning a promiscuous adventure (rather than that he was instinctively drawn to look at an attractive female). Again, this clarification of the difference between her previously established pattern of the use of promiscuity to restore self-esteem and her partner's reflex looking at other women provided her with some relief.

The man who was not jealous

Some years ago I saw a chronically depressed man—Mr W—whose self-esteem and self-image were negative in the extreme. He rather floridly spoke of his view of himself as the "lowest of the low" and of his place at "the bottom of the ladder", and described himself as "a zero—a nothing". He also frequently referred to himself as "a twat"—a widely used derogatory term that originally is slang for female genitals. Mr W talked of his view that most other men were more intelligent than him, as well as being more attractive to women and generally more able. Although educated to a high level, he said he had not been able to progress in his career beyond the first rung. His generally submissive and deferential stance was apparent in relation to me—for example, he would ask permission to remove his jacket on an extremely hot day. Mr W was so emphatic about his general worthlessness and his inferiority compared to other men that I began to suspect his low self-esteem was serving a defensive function of placing him outside the arena of potential competition with other men. This hypothesis began to make sense in terms of what emerged of his early Oedipal situation. Mr W's biological father had left when he was in his first year and he had no conscious memories of him. Until age five he had his mother to himself. However, she then married a man from a quite different race and culture, whom Mr W experienced as "a fierce stranger" and utterly terrifying. It was apparent from Mr W's recollections that he had feared greatly for his physical safety if he provoked his stepfather's anger. Thus it seemed likely that Mr W's Oedipal wishes to remain close to his mother and to eliminate the "fierce stranger" rival would have been a source of considerable anxiety, resulting in a wholesale repudiation of his competitive strivings and the adoption of extreme submission behaviour—his self-denigratory thoughts being an *internal* form of submission behaviour. Mr W was startled by this interpretation, but found it meaningful. He talked of how he always wore an old tie that was thin and frayed—claiming that his self-esteem was so low that he did not feel he deserved a "wide" tie of the kind that most men would wear. He felt this was a "signal" to other men that he was at the bottom of the pecking order or, as he rather histrionically put it, he was "no higher than microbes on the floor". The phallic symbolism of the tie was obvious—it was as if he was displaying a visual statement that his penis was "thin" and of no competitive threat. His frequent reference to himself as a "twat" similarly declared his presentation of himself as castrated and therefore having no rival phallus.

Alongside Mr W's fear of evoking retaliation for any potential competitive strivings, there was another anxiety of a more narcissistic nature. It became apparent that his self-mockery and expressions of extreme contempt for himself were attempts to ensure that his abilities could never be overestimated by his colleagues or by anyone else with whom he came into contact. By presenting himself as the "lowest of the low" he endeavoured to prevent the possibility of being given a task which might be beyond his capacities. In this way he pre-empted the possibility of what would be experienced by him as catastrophic humiliation and shame if he were to fail. Thus he found narcissistic safety in his exaggeratedly low self-esteem.

Mr W did have a girlfriend, although he felt he was of no value to her and did not see why she stayed with him. In view of his low self-esteem and image of himself as undesirable, I expected him to experience strong feelings of jealous anxiety that his girlfriend would turn to other men. To my surprise Mr W completely denied any jealousy initially. It was as if he felt that should his girlfriend leave him this would be only what he deserved—and would therefore be an event to accept stoically and without resistance. His absence of jealousy seemed to reflect his having placed himself entirely outside the realm of competition with other men. However, as Mr W's defences against his Oedipal strivings were explored he suddenly began to speak of his desire for a very attractive woman at work and his hatred, envy, and jealousy of her high-achieving husband who headed the company, and whom he regarded as having everything that Mr W wanted—intelligence, ability, confidence, success, and a beautiful wife. It was apparent that, behind his exaggerated self-mockery and opting out of competition and placing himself at the bottom of the pecking order, lay the opposite feelings and (Oedipal) fantasies—of being the *most successful* man with the most beautiful wife. Whilst initially repudiated, his feelings of jealousy were powerfully albeit latently present.

One striking feature of Mr W's presentation was how his particular constellation of repudiation of competition was entwined with extreme forms of shame. He illustrated vividly the process whereby shame leads to retreat down the social hierarchy—this retreat, when taken beyond a certain socially acceptable point, becomes itself a source of shame, thus giving rise to toxic shame and the sense of being unfit for human society. At the deepest biological level, the shame concerns being reproductively unfit.

Freud's insights regarding jealousy

Freud's main contribution specifically concerning jealousy was his

1922 paper, "Some neurotic mechanisms in jealousy, paranoia and homosexuality". He states his view that normal jealousy is ubiquitous and is derived from both the current situation and, unconsciously from the childhood Oedipal situation and sibling rivalry. It combines grief, narcissistic injury (to self-esteem) and self-criticism:

> It is easy to see that essentially it is compounded of grief, the pain caused by the thought of losing the loved object, and of the narcissistic wound, in so far as this is distinguishable from the other wound; further of feelings of enmity against the successful rival, and of a greater or lesser amount of self-criticism which tries to hold the subject's own ego accountable for his loss. Although we may call it normal, this jealousy is by no means completely rational, that is, derived from the actual situation, proportionate to the real circumstances and under the complete control of the conscious ego; for it is rooted deep in the unconscious, it is a continuation of the earliest stirrings of the child's affective life, and it originates in the Oedipus or brother-and-sister complex of the first sexual period. [Freud, 1922, p. 223]

Here he describes a variety of pathological forms of jealousy deriving from projection and related mechanisms of defence. Freud argues that projected jealousy is common, deriving from a person's denial and projection of his or her own impulses to be unfaithful. He comments:

> It is a matter of everyday experience that fidelity, especially that degree of it required in marriage, is only maintained in the face of continual temptations. Anyone who denies these temptations in himself will nevertheless feel their pressure so strongly that he will be glad enough to make use of an unconscious mechanism to alleviate his situation. He can obtain this alleviation—and indeed acquittal by his conscience—if he projects his own impulses to faithlessness on to the partner to whom he owes faith. [Freud, 1922, p. 224]

Normally, Freud points out, social convention tolerates mild degrees of flirtation outside marriage, so that the "inevitable tendency to unfaithfulness will thus find a safety valve and be rendered innocuous" [p. 224]. However, the pathologically jealous person does not tolerate such flirtation, appearing to believe that it will inevitably lead to actual infidelity. The force of this conviction derives from the projection, which will always find some justification because of the inevitability of some degree of temptation in the partner to be unfaithful. The jealous person does not project where there is no suitable match:

> They let themselves be guided by their knowledge of the unconscious, and displace to the unconscious minds of others the attention which they have withdrawn from their own. Our jealous husband perceived his wife's unfaithfulness instead of his own; by becoming conscious of hers and magnifying it enormously he succeeded in keeping his own unconscious. [Freud, 1922, p. 226]

A more serious kind of delusional jealousy arises from projection not merely of impulses to be unfaithful *per se*, but also of repressed *homosexual* impulses:

> As an attempt at defence against an unduly strong homosexual impulse it may, in a man, be described in the formula: "*I* do not love him, *she* loves him". [Freud, 1922, p. 225]

Of course the equivalent process may occur in a woman. In one case told to the author, a woman experienced intense and painful jealousy in her heterosexual relationships, continually alert to any indication or possibility of her partner's infidelity—but this tendency to be jealous faded considerably once she had acknowledged her homosexuality and had settled into a lesbian relationship.

However, Freud also described a contrasting process whereby intense jealousy in childhood can give rise to homosexuality. This is rather the reverse of the process whereby homosexuality gives rise to jealousy. In such instances the young boy had a strong attachment to the mother and intense jealous rivalry against brothers, involving death wishes. Eventually this hostility succumbed to repression and underwent a transformation, such that the original rivals then became the first homosexual love-objects. This transformation of hate into love is quite opposite to the process Freud described for paranoia, in which repudiation of love for a same sex figure undergoes repression and transformation into hatred. Freud suggested that the transformation of rivalrous hatred into love may often occur after the mother has praised another rival boy.

An example of jealousy based on projection

It is not hard to find examples illustrating Freud's formulation of jealousy based on projection. One woman demonstrated this rather vividly, and also showed how a cycle of jealousy can be self-reinforcing. She described how she would, at times, enter states of delusional and intense jealousy, continually checking to see whether her husband was seeing other women, and scarcely containing herself from bursting in on his place of work in order to catch him in his supposed infidelities. Initially she rebuffed the analyst's enquiry into her own possible wishes to be unfaithful—but then confessed that recently she had indeed found herself thinking a lot about her previous boyfriend, whom she actually regretted having left. She had heard that he was getting married, although she knew that he had continued to pine for her long after she had left him. Whilst she recognized that both their lives had moved on, she nevertheless found herself contemplating how life might have been if she had stayed with him. Such thoughts evoked considerable guilt and anxiety, for she loved her husband and was devoted to her children that she now had with him. The analyst put to her that she may have been dealing with her feelings of guilt and anxiety about her secret thoughts about her previous boyfriend (her internal affair) by projectively attributing them to her husband—"it is not me who wants to be unfaithful but him". Once this was put to her, the patient could see very clearly how this was the case. It was then possible to understand how her cycle of jealousy could be self-reinforcing: her projection onto her husband of her own impulses to be unfaithful meant that she felt insecure with him; this insecurity made her more inclined to fantasize about the life she could have had with her previous boyfriend; her anxiety and guilt about such thoughts and impulses gave rise to increased projection, resulting in increased insecurity—and so on in a positive feedback loop. A related loop—one which is common in cycles of jealousy—was that, as she tormented her husband with her jealousy, she felt sure she must be driving him away from her through her intolerable behaviour, which then increased her suspicion that he would want

[handwritten margin notes: "o/D ✓ Riviere — jealousy linked to early greed & envy — wish to possess all & spoil what others have"]

to turn to another woman—which fuelled her jealous rage, which she felt sure would lead him to reject her—and so on.

Riviere's elaboration of Freud's formulation of jealousy

In a remarkable paper in 1932, Joan Riviere elaborated on Freud's insights into the projective processes involved in jealousy, showing the deeper and earlier—"pre-Oedipal"—forms of greed and envy that lay behind a woman patient's jealous preoccupations. These were seen as deriving from the relationship to the primal scene of the parental relationship and to sadistic wishes to deprive the parents of all their possessions and gratifications.

She described the case of a young married woman who sought analysis because of a lack of response during intercourse and also certain inhibitions. The jealousy arose as a transitory symptom during the analysis—taking the form of suspicions that her husband was having affairs and also beliefs that her husband had written letters to the analyst. Riviere found that although the patient herself showed some tendencies to be flirtatious, these did not seem plausibly to be the basis of her jealousy since she talked about her flirtations quite openly. Instead, Riviere noticed that the patient would indulge in outbursts of self-condemnation regarding her flirtations whenever, in the previous session, there had been some new insight into her unconscious life—giving rise to the hypothesis that her guilt about her own impulses towards infidelity were serving some defensive purpose in relation to the analysis. Nevertheless, the patient's jealousy was at times so persecutory in character that Riviere was convinced that *something* was being projected, even if it was unclear what.

Eventually Riviere was able to elucidate "a specific unconscious phantasy-situation which took shape in her life in ever-varying forms". This "dominant phantasy" consisted of "an impulse or an act on the patient's part of seizing and obtaining from some other person something she greatly desired, thus robbing and despoiling him or her". Whilst her conscious wish was to win the love of her husband, children, and all those around her, what this "love" meant to her was that they would surrender completely to her, in such a way that they would give up all rights and possibilities of pleasure

Cf. jealousy & shame

for themselves. In her flirtations she wanted to rob another woman of her husband and the pleasures he gave her. She wanted the analyst's husband to die and also wanted to possess him herself. For her, all pleasures had to be at some other person's expense. In every situation she had to be in a preferential position over others. Her envy of the analyst was masked by an attitude of contempt that became the prevailing mood in the transference. Riviere concluded that it was whenever there was a danger that the unconscious phantasy might be realized, especially in some bodily way relating to sexuality, illness or death, the patient's anxiety would develop to an extent that it could be relieved only by projection of the impulses:

> So in the jealous moods she declared that her husband and his other women were robbing her of everything, taunting, outraging her, stripping her of his love, of her own self-respect and self-confidence, casting her off, a victim, utterly helpless and destitute. But this was precisely what in countless ways, as in her flirtations, she was unconsciously endeavouring to do to all around her. [p. 419]

Riviere described the patient's recurrent masturbation phantasy which captured the unconscious desire: A young girl is in a doctor's consulting room, being undressed and then examined by him; there is another woman in the background. The analysis revealed that the doctor represented her father, whilst the woman in the background stood for the mother to be robbed and despoiled. In line with Riviere's Kleinian theoretical framework, she saw the patient's desire as being to rob the mother of her body contents:

> ... the mother was, as one might say, a double object in herself, consisting of two parts: namely herself and her possessions; the father (or his penis, the agent) was one of her possessions, of which she was to be robbed. The mother's possessions consisted ultimately of her breasts, milk and her body-contents: faeces, children and the father's penis; of all these she was to be despoiled. [p. 420]

Riviere reasoned that "simple genital Oedipus desire and jealousy" played little part in the patient's phantasies. Instead these were rooted in envy and sadistic impulses from the early oral phase of development, wherein others were regarded not as whole persons but as "part objects": "Men were not really persons and full objects to the patient's unconscious; a man was either a penis or was the owner of a penis. Women were also part-objects, i.e. apprehended as divisible into part-objects" (p. 420). Riviere suggested that this unconscious perception of others as part objects contributed to the relative indifference shown by such patients to the actual personalities of others. One further point made by Riviere was that the bitterness of the jealous person's preoccupation with real or imagined infidelities on the part of their spouse is that unconsciously these are imagined as retributions for his or her own aggressive intentions during early childhood.

Fenichel's contribution

Another important early paper was that of Otto Fenichel in 1935, in which he draws upon some of the points made by Riviere[5] and, like her, gives an example of a patient who had unconsciously wished to rob her mother.

Fenichel begins with two puzzling features of jealousy. First, he makes the point that jealousy is not necessarily strongest where a previous state of love has been greatest—and that, in fact, those who are most inclined to be jealous may often be those who are incapable of deeper forms of love and who change their love-objects continually. Secondly, he notes that another surprising feature of jealousy is that it tends to be an obtrusive and supervalent idea.

Regarding the first point, Fenichel argues that those prone to jealousy tend to be "orally fixated" people whose self-esteem is unusually dependent upon receiving love—an external locus of self-esteem. This need to take in "narcissistic supplies" from the environment is similar to that shown by depressive and other patients with "oral" or "self-regarding" neuroses—as described originally by Rado (1928).

Fenichel relates this narcissistic quality to the role of unconscious homosexuality—drawing upon Freud's hypothesis regarding projected homosexual impulses in delusional jealousy and paranoia. He postulates that the use of projection and the homosexual object choice are both archaic and narcissistic:

... projection ... which characterises the paranoid mechanisms contained in jealousy, is an archaic mechanism which points to the persistence of a relatively narcissistic stage. The homosexual object is closer to the narcissistic object, that is to the subject's own ego, than is the heterosexual object. [p. 352]

Fenichel's clinical example

Fenichel gives a clinical example. A middle aged woman relapsed into a severe neurosis characterized by anxiety, depersonalization and hysterical conversion symptoms. Initially she reported that the symptoms had arisen after her husband had become impotent. However, it later emerged that her symptoms had arisen only after she had begun to suspect that her husband was seeing another woman and she had developed the conviction that he would be fully potent with her rival. Her symptoms thus arose in the context of "an intense and torturing jealousy which until then had been quite unknown to her". Moreover, it transpired that she herself had often been sexually unresponsive to her husband and had never been particularly keen on intercourse with him, relying instead on periodic masturbation with particular fantasies.

The patient rapidly developed a demanding attitude towards the analyst, showing distinctly "oral" incorporative qualities. For example, she declared that it was only when the analyst talked to her that she felt worthy of respect and that after analytic hours when she felt he had not talked enough she would visit a pastry shop and consume a cake. Without the narcissistic supplies from the analyst to "maintain" her, as she put it, she experienced anxiety, depersonalization and feelings of worthlessness. (In the more contemporary terms of Kohutian self-psychology, this would be described as a mirroring transference, in which the analyst is required to function as a "selfobject"—i.e. to function as part of the patient's narcissistic economy.)

During the analysis the patient's jealousy increased, taking the form of torturing thoughts about when and where and how he might be seeing the other woman, with compulsive fantasies of their sexual intimacy. Eventually she declared that she could not tolerate having to think of her husband "giving his penis" to another woman. Fenichel concluded that she thought of her husband's penis, unconsciously, as a source of oral supplies of the kind she sought from the analyst—the attention and interest that bolstered her self-esteem through the supply of words. However, the point was striking that she did not feel deprived of such supplies simply by her husband's impotence, but by the idea of another woman receiving what she did not.

A relevant part of the background was that the patient's father had an affair with a maid and when the mother discovered this she had poured her heart out to the patient. Therefore, Fenichel reasoned that the patient's situation with her husband related to the repressed Oedipus complex:

> The thought that her husband might be with another woman was intolerable because the husband, by being unfaithful, became a father-figure. The patient, afraid of retribution, felt: "Now I get what as a child, identifying myself with the maid, I did to my mother." [p. 356]

However, Fenichel pointed to deeper sources of what emerged as the patient's conception of sexual intercourse as "a robbing of what is not given freely". Apparently, at puberty a girl friend told her of seeing a farm labourer having sex with a girl standing up. This image became a persisting source of great excitement for the patient—and from then on, her masturbation fantasies always pivoted around there being a woman watching a couple having intercourse—with the detail that the man had left the watching woman for the other woman. Fenichel considered that the patient's excitement required that she empathize simultaneously with both women—"with the robber and the robbed one". This could then be linked with her "split" feeling associated with her experience of depersonalization—"she was split into a robber-woman and a robbed woman". Fenichel concluded:

> The unconscious masturbation fantasies which had been reinforced by the husband's unfaithfulness may be formulated more or less as follows: "I want to take my father from my mother, as the maid did. When I have a husband, what happened to my mother will happen to me." [p. 356]

Consciously the patient hated both her mother and her sister. She reproached her mother for almost everything—and Fenichel deduced that the formula for these disappointments in her mother must have been: "She had taken something from me to give it to others". The theme of robbery and of one woman taking from another woman became more pronounced, based around the unconscious idea: "I take another woman's food away from her" or "If they take my food away, I will get it back by robbing (my mother's body)" (p. 357). As the analysis continued, memories emerged of childhood kleptomania. She recalled stealing chess pieces from her father and throwing them into the toilet—and then remembered doing the same with various belongings of her mother. Fenichel linked these actions with her hatred against her younger sister "whom—in accordance with an anal theory of birth—she had wanted to remove again in this fashion". He concluded: "The meaning of all these actions was: "I get for myself what is withheld from me. I take revenge for the love that was taken from me. I want to get back what I lost" (p. 357). At one point in the analysis, during discussion of a dream relating to anal impulses of childhood, the patient suddenly hallucinated an intensely strong taste and knew that this was the taste of faeces. Fenichel concluded that although the patient could not remember doing so, "there could be no doubt that she had engaged in coprophagic activities in order to "get back what she had lost' " (p. 358).

Fenichel's overall understanding of his patient's jealousy was that it was based on oral–sadistic wishes to rob her mother. When her early relationship with her mother had been disturbed by the arrival of her sister, her first reaction had not been to turn to her father but to become fixated to a fantasy: "I am being robbed and I rob". This fixation had been enhanced at puberty by, first of all, the stimulation of her Oedipus complex by her father's involvement with the maid, and then her girl friend's story of the voyeur scene— a story which easily acted as a "screen experience" for the more or less contemporary situation of her father and the maid, and her fantasies about this. Fenichel concluded:

> Her jealousy, her feeling that any triangular situation was intolerable, and yet having always to think of such a situation, corresponds to an attempt to repress her own oral sadism and nevertheless to gratify it. The motive of her repression was fear of retribution. This was naturally reinforced when the patient felt that she had *actually* been robbed of something. [p. 358]

Klein - excellent
distinct betw.
jealousy & envy

Melanie Klein's contribution

Melanie Klein's made a substantial contribution to the understanding of jealousy in what is arguably her finest paper—"Envy
and gratitude" (1957). Drawing upon Abraham's view that envy is
an "oral" character trait, she describes some of the early expressions
of envy in the infant's relationship to the breast and the feeding
mother, and outlines how it forms the basis of jealousy. Klein
believed that the infant's relationship to the breast formed the basis
of feelings of security:

> Under the dominance of oral impulses, the breast is instinctively felt
> to be the source of nourishment and therefore in a deeper sense, of
> life itself. This mental and physical closeness to the gratifying breast
> in some measure restores, if things go well, the lost prenatal unity
> with the mother and the feeling of security that goes with it.
> [pp. 178–179]

She described how a variety of external factors can interfere with
the infant's relationship to the breast, including difficulties at birth,
the quality of the mother's care and feeding, and the mother's state
of mind. However, in this paper, Klein particularly emphasized the
role of envy in impeding the relationship to the breast. She distinguished between envy and jealousy as follows:

> Envy is the angry feeling that another person possesses and enjoys
> something desirable—the envious impulse being to take it away or
> to spoil it. Moreover, envy implies the subject's relation to one
> person only and goes back to the earliest exclusive relation with the
> mother. Jealousy is based on envy, but involves a relation to at least
> two people; it is mainly concerned with love that the subject feels is
> his due and has been taken away, or is in danger of being taken
> away, from him by his rival. In the everyday conception of jealousy,
> a man or a woman feels deprived of the loved person by somebody
> else. [p. 181]

Klein linked envy with greed. She described the latter as "an
impetuous and insatiable craving, exceeding what the subject needs
and what the object is able and willing to give", which "aims
primarily at completely scooping out, sucking dry, and devouring
the breast", whereas "envy not only seeks to rob in this way, but
also to put badness, primarily bad excrements and bad parts of the

self into the mother, and first of all into her breast, in order to spoil and destroy her" (p. 181). Klein drew attention to the expression "to bite the hand that feeds", which captures the idea of attacking the breast out of envy of its goodness and capacity to feed. In jealousy there is a fear of losing that which is loved, whereas in envy the good object is itself attacked. Klein quotes Crabb's English Synonyms: "The envious man sickens at the sight of enjoyment. He is easy only in the misery of others" (Klein, p. 182). She notes that envy is classed amongst the "seven deadly sins", and comments, "I would even suggest that it is unconsciously felt to be the greatest sin of all, because it spoils and harms the good object which is the source of life" (p. 189).

Klein argued that jealousy arises out of the original envy towards the feeding breast, and forms part of the early Oedipal situation: "Jealousy is based on the suspicion of and rivalry with the father, who is accused of having taken away the mother's breast and the mother" (p. 196). She adds that disturbances in the early relationship to the mother, because of environmental factors or the strength of envy, complicates the rivalry with the father in the Oedipal situation:

> The development of the Oedipus complex is strongly influenced by the vicissitudes of the first exclusive relation with the mother, and when this relation is disturbed too soon, the rivalry with the father enters prematurely. Phantasies of the penis inside the mother, or inside her breast, turn the father into a hostile intruder. This phantasy is particularly strong when the infant has not had the full enjoyment and happiness that the early relation to the mother can afford him and has not taken in the first good object with some security. Such a failure partly depends on the strength of envy. [p. 197]

She describes how the phantasy of the mother's breast or body containing the father's penis, or of the father containing the breast or the mother, form the basis of a common phantasy of the "combined parents". This is particularly provocative of envy because the parents are then felt to be in continuous intercourse and providing each other with never-ending pleasurable sexual gratification. However, when envy is not too excessive, Oedipal jealousy can become a means of modifying it because the hostility then is directed at a rival (the father or siblings) so that one figure is still loved:

With the boy, a good deal of hate is deflected onto the father who is envied for the possession of the mother; this is the typical Oedipus jealousy. With the girl, the genital desires for the father enable her to find another loved object. Thus jealousy to some extent supersedes envy; the mother becomes the chief rival. The girl desires to take her mother's place and to possess and take care of the babies which the loved father gives to the mother. The identification with the mother in this role makes a wider range of sublimations possible. It is essential also to consider that the working-through of envy by means of jealousy is at the same time a defence against envy. Jealousy is felt to be much more acceptable and gives rise much less to guilt than the primary envy which destroys the first good object. [p. 198]

However, she argued that if the little girl's turning to the father is driven by excessive envy of the mother—a rivalry that is "much less due to love of the father than to envy of the mother's possession of the father and his penis"—then the father is seen as an appendage to the mother and the desire is to rob her mother of this. Klein explained how this may become a pervasive and repeating pattern:

Therefore in later life, every success in her relation to men becomes a victory over another woman. ... If the man is mainly valued because his conquest is a triumph over another woman, she may lose interest in him as soon as success has been achieved. The attitude towards the rival woman then implies: "You (standing for the mother) had that wonderful breast which I could not get when you withheld it from me and which I still wish to rob you of; therefore I take from you that penis which you cherish." The need to repeat this triumph over a hated rival often strongly contributes to the search for another and yet another man. [p. 200]

Thus Klein describes how jealousy, when based on envy, gives rise to the wish to rob the rival, who originally represents the mother. When this wish to rob is projected, then the jealous person lives in continual fear of being robbed by a rival.

Early origins of jealousy

The validity of Freud's view of jealousy arising in the two

constellations of, first, the child's triangular Oedipal rivalry and, second, his or her resentment of siblings, can readily be found in everyday observation of children. Whilst Oedipal rivalry may be slightly more hidden (but not very much), hatred of siblings is usually quite overt and obvious. Mitchell (2000) has recently argued that the role of sibling jealousy in personality development has tended to be relatively neglected within psychoanalysis.

Wisdom (1976) describes the case of a twelve-month-old boy who developed anxiety, nightmares, intolerance of separation from his mother, and a fear of strangers, after a baby brother was born. His overt reactions to being shown the baby oscillated markedly between two contrasting attitudes—of smiling with delight and of displaying dismay and apparent bewilderment. When the boy awoke from his nightmares he could not easily be soothed by the parents. After a while, a different tactic was adopted. The baby's cradle would be brought into the presence of the boy—with the result that he immediately became calm. Whilst this reaction seems, on the face of it, somewhat puzzling, the author hypothesizes that the presence of the baby acted as a reassurance, first, that he had not been harmed by the boy's hostile phantasies, and, second, that the baby did not have a privileged place with the mother. After seeing the baby, the boy would express pleasure, but then turn away and demand contact with the mother. His attitude towards his mother showed ambivalence, however, since he would sometimes bite her severely. He also displayed some signs of regression—such as, sleeping in a position he had previously abandoned, liking to climb on his mother's breast in a way he had not done for some months, liking to lie in his mother's arm when feeding, and becoming less resistant to nappies.

Another development was that during the day he liked to spend as much time as possible with his father, to the exclusion of other people, but then at night this was reversed and he would only be interested in his mother. The author speculates that this expressed the little boy's Oedipal wish to take in as much as possible of his father in order to repossess his mother:

> Assuming that his basic need now was to make sure of having his mother as the main object of his attachment, in his day-time activities he could best achieve this goal upon Oedipus theory by

absorbing as much of his father as he could; indeed it was noted
how remarkable it was to see him making imitative movements of
his father driving the car and trying to use a shovel to get coal out of
a coalscuttle to put on the fire; through this introjective identification he would feel restored and would try to get back his mother in
the evening. [Wisdom, 1976, p. 367]

Yet another aspect of the little boy's attempts to adapt to his
feelings of jealousy was shown in evidence of identification with the
mother and to relate to the baby as if it were his own child. For
example, he would try to brush the baby's hair and put away the
hairbrush in the way that his mother did.

By four weeks after the baby's birth, there was an observation
suggesting that the boy had come to terms with his jealousy partly
by transforming this into tender feelings and a concern to protect
the baby. The brothers were out in the garden, one in a carry-cot
and the other in a pram; the baby awoke and began whimpering;
the older boy began screaming loudly until one of the parents came
and attended to the baby, which then restored calm to both. This
happened three times—and on the third occasion the boy actually
pointed to the baby. When the baby was taken indoors, the boy
remained happily outside alone.

Jealousy and envy

Jealousy and envy are often confused—and indeed do seem to have
overlapping meanings. In a paper attempting to clarify these
meanings, Spielman (1971) comments that the two words are often
used interchangeably or in conjunction with one another—and that
"even the same colour, green, is associated with both emotions, as
in the popular phrase 'green with envy' and in Shakespeare's
Othello: 'jealousy—the green-eyed monster'" (p. 59). On the whole,
envy is regarded as the more primitive and simpler emotion—a
wish to possess what the other has. However some authors, such as
Klein (1957) consider that envy also may contain the wish that the
other person not have the desired thing or quality, whilst others
describe this as an attribute of jealousy. Thus Spielman (1971) states:
"envy bespeaks the desire to have what someone else has; jealousy

is this as well as wanting the other person not to have it" (p. 59). He goes on to describe envy as follows:

> In envy one is unhappy that another person possesses something one would like to have for oneself and feels inferior because of not having it. This may be a thing, a person, or both; or it may be a quality such as success, reputation, or happiness. Envy may also include admiration of the envied thing or person, covetousness towards the envied thing, hatred or resentment of the person possessing the envied thing, a wish to harm the envied person, and, perhaps, a wish to rob the person of the envied thing. Crucial to the definition is that the interpersonal configuration is a two-person one in which the other person has possession of that which is envied. [p. 60]

Regarding jealousy, he comments:

> In jealousy one experiences apprehension, anxiety, suspicion, or mistrust concerning the loss of a highly valued possession, or the diversion to another, a third person, of affection and love. It is often associated with an attitude of vigilant guarding against the threatened loss and an effort to preserve the status quo, to maintain possession. In sexual love this might involve an attempt to exact exclusive devotion from the love object. The possession, or valued "good", in jealousy tends to be a person or the affection of a person rather than an inanimate object or quality, but this is not always so. Rivalry with a third person is typically involved and highlights a crucial aspect of jealousy; it occurs in a three-person situation in which the jealous person fears a third person will intrude upon a two-person relationship and take possession. [p. 61]

Thus Spielman emphasizes the distinction between envy and jealousy primarily in terms of whether it is a two-person or three-person situation. However, he sees jealousy as the more complex emotion, which contains envy as a component. Jealousy includes a sense of loss or threat of loss, which is not inherent in envy. Also the jealous person may be more inclined towards self-blame for failures (e.g. in losing a lover to a rival). In addition, jealousy, especially in its more pathological forms, may include elements of projection of the person's own disavowed heterosexual, homosexual, and hostile wishes. This projection may also contribute to a paranoid trend in jealous individuals.

"Penis envy"

Freud referred to envy only in his concept of penis envy:

> If we penetrate deeply enough into the neurosis of a woman, we not infrequently meet with the repressed wish to possess a penis like a man. We call this wish "envy for a penis" and include it in the castration complex. [Freud, 1917, p. 129]

In an earlier work on children's sexual theories, Freud describes the origins of this envy:

> It is easy to observe that little girls fully share their brother's opinion of it. They develop a great interest in that part of the boy's body. But this interest promptly falls under the sway of envy. They feel themselves unfairly treated. They make attempts to micturate in the posture that is made possible for the boys by their possessing a big penis; and when a girl declares that "she would rather be a boy", we know what deficiency her wish is intended to put right. [Freud, 1908, p. 218]

Although this notion has been much debated (e.g. Gallup, 1982; Mitchell, 1974; Torok, 1970), it may sometimes emerge in a rather clear and obvious way in the case of women who have felt that brothers were favoured because of their gender. For example, one woman always felt that her birth had been a great disappointment to her parents because they had wanted a boy. She felt that nothing she did was ever of interest or pleasure to her parents. When her younger brother was born she perceived that, by contrast, they clearly were delighted with him. She noticed that he possessed an organ between his legs, like the one she had observed on her father. This highly visible piece of anatomy was the only obvious physical difference between them—and therefore it seemed to her, in her child mind, that this must be the reason why he was loved and she was not. The penis then readily came to symbolize for her all the advantages, power, and love that she felt were unfairly bestowed on males. Her lack of the phallus (as it might be termed in its symbolic function) was a focus of deep feelings of shame and inadequacy.[6] Of course it is not the actual organ that is envied, but what it is felt to represent. Torok (1970) comments: "Penis envy is always envy of an idealised penis. ... It is obvious that this always means: 'the thing whatever it is that one doesn't have oneself'" (p. 139).

Envy, jealousy and shame

Envy, jealousy, and shame are intimately related. Shame reflects our sense of being disconnected, separate, inferior, misunderstood, or excluded—and then envy and jealousy may closely follow. In a panel discussion of these three emotions, Reisenberg-Malcolm (reported by De Paola, 2001) described a patient who experienced shame whenever the analyst said something about which he had not thought before, reacting like a person stabbed. This painful experience of shame appeared to be triggered by a feeling that an infantile state of oneness with the analyst in the transference had been "cut", so that the patient was then confronted with the reality that the source of the interpretations was the analyst; at such moments he would feel separate and inferior. At other times, the same patient would display envy and jealousy whenever he was confronted with his lack of exclusive ownership of the analyst whom he could potentially experience as a needed and longed-for figure. Jealousy would express his wish for an exclusive relationship, whilst envy would lead him to adopt an aloof and triumphant–contemptuous stance.

In the same panel discussion, Morrison and Lansky pointed to the way in which envy, contempt, and shame are all concerned with comparison of self to other. In envy the other is exalted and hated, whilst in contempt the other is despised and lowered in comparison with an exalted self. If envy is consciously experienced, then it is accompanied by shame, which Morrison and Lansky view as the core emotion in negative self-evaluation. Shame can function as a warning of threats to connection with the other and can initiate attempts to repair or restore the bond; on the other hand, envy and contempt represent attempts to remove oneself from the other's power to threaten rejection or loss. In this way, Morrison and Lansky view envy and contempt as expressions of a shame-derived *vision* of the "death instinct", Thanatos—a protective withdrawal from needed figures; they contrasted this with a Kleinian view of envy as a form of primary aggression *emanating* from Thanatos (De Paola, 2001).

Thus shame erupts when a gulf arises between self and other—a disruption of empathy, understanding, acceptance, or attunement—resulting then in an evaluation of self as lacking or inferior in some way. Closely following shame may be envy, as the other is perceived as desired, separate, and unavailable. Jealousy may come into play as more favoured rivals are seen as potentially taking the place of intimacy with the other, from which the self has been ejected. Contempt and devaluation of the other may be a defence against shame, envy, and jealousy.

Jealousy based on valid unconscious perception

It is not uncommon for those in the listening professions to hear a person berating him or herself for their excessive jealousy and suspicion of their spouse, only to learn later that the partner was indeed being unfaithful. The "jealous" one had attempted to disavow their accurate perceptions and intuitions, preferring to believe that they were suffering from pathological or unfounded jealousy, especially if this was the "explanation" offered by the unfaithful partner. This is illustrated vividly in the findings of one psychiatrist who specialized in work with couples where one partner displayed "morbid jealousy". Often the husband would appear to be suffering delusions of jealousy. Since the psychiatrist believed that such jealousy was an incurable psychiatric condition, he often advised the couples to separate or divorce. However, he routinely followed up his patients after some months. He was surprised to discover that many of the wives had subsequently become openly involved with the very men about whom the husbands had been jealous. Thus the "delusional" husband must have been accurately registering signs of infidelity, but because this was denied by the wife, he would conclude that the idea was irrational and that he required psychiatric help (reported by Buss, 2000).

A male patient in analysis with the author described tormenting anxiety and feelings of jealousy after the woman he loved reported receiving a phone call from a man she had met in a nightclub. The woman assured him that whilst she had engaged in kissing this man whilst drunk at the nightclub, she had no serious emotional or sexual interest in him. The patient felt perturbed because, although she had acknowledged going to the nightclub, the woman had initially denied having given the man her phone number. Not surprisingly, he struggled with a sense of uncertainty about the situation and tried to convey to the woman the intense and anguished nature of his jealousy and his fantasies of her sexual infidelity. She protested that his jealous fantasies were extremely destructive to their relationship and pleaded with him to try to keep these in check. The patient endeavoured to put aside his strong intuitive sense that the woman had already had sex with the man from the nightclub. He tried to rest in the woman's assurance of her love for him and his desire to trust her. Indeed he knew that she tended compulsively and impulsively to have short-lived lustful preoccupations and brief sexual adventures which did not include emotional involvement—and whilst he did not like these, he tolerated them. She insisted that her heart and her love remained firmly and deeply with him. All of this background added to his feeling of devastation and betrayal when the woman eventually confessed some time later that she had indeed become seriously sexually and emotionally involved with the nightclub man—and that she had engaged in considerable deception about this. Because the patient had indeed trusted her, and had wanted to dismiss his anxieties as pathological jealousy and a sign of his inability to trust, he was profoundly shocked and traumatized when the truth emerged. He was left feeling that he could not trust anything the woman had ever said to him—and nor could he trust his own judgement. His ensuing symptoms of post-traumatic stress disorder were quite marked—with anxiety, depression, suicidal preoccupations, sleep disturbance, and intrusive flashback images of the woman's confession of infidelity. In the analysis it was possible to link these reactions to his infantile experience when his mother had become depressed and withdrawn during his second year of life following a stillbirth (an event which he had been told about but could not, of course, remember directly). It seemed likely that this early experience had predisposed him to be very alert to indications of a woman's degree of emotional involvement or withdrawal from him—and to link withdrawal in some way with the idea of a rival for the woman's emotional attention. Thus his perceptions of his friend's withdrawal and infidelity, her sexual fantasies, and her state of mind in relation to him, were probably highly accurate—but disavowed in response to her wish to deny them and his wish to believe her.

Another patient reported to his analyst (not the author) that he had the impression that a friend, also in analysis with the same analyst, was having an affair since he had seen her with another man at a concert. The analyst, concerned about preserving confidentiality, emphasized to the patient that he was making unwarranted inferences from the evidence—that all he had seen was the woman in the company of another man, but this did not mean that she was having an affair. When it later emerged that the patient's inference had been entirely correct he felt angry that the analyst had, in effect, invalidated his accurate perception. He felt, probably correctly, that this had been done in order to reduce the analyst's anxiety about dangers of potential breaches of confidentiality.

A related phenomenon may arise from a childhood attempt to disavow accurate perceptions of being unloved. A woman talked of her continual doubts about her partner's love and fidelity. She continually accused him of having affairs and would fly into rages triggered by her suspicions. At other moments she would severely condemn herself for her "irrational" jealousy. In exploring her childhood experiences, what emerged was that she had never felt convinced of her mother's love for her. It seemed that she had in fact often perceived her mother as subtly withdrawn and hostile towards her—but, when asked, her mother would always assure her that she did love her. The patient wanted to believe her mother's assertion of love, but to do so meant that she had to disavow her (probably accurate) perception of her mother's hostility. At times she would be in an intolerable state of confusion about whether she was loved or hated—and this confusion would be evoked regularly in relation to her adult partner. Eventually it became clear that her partner was in fact unfaithful—and so in this way too her pattern of attempting to disavow her accurate but disturbing perceptions repeated the childhood experience.

As a general principle, it appears that if one party to a relationship, whether this be a parent or an adult partner, professes love for the other, but that other person perceives this not to be the case, sensing instead indications of hostility, infidelity or betrayal, there is then a situation that can evoke intense distress, anxiety, and confusion. The wish to believe the protestation of love is in competition with the perception (whether conscious or unconscious) that this is not true (Freyd, 1996)—and the ensuing sense of confusion can severely undermine a person's grasp of reality and confidence in their own judgement. It is the problem of accurate perception or intuition being invalidated as paranoia.

Fenichel's example of unconscious perception

Fenichel (1926) gives and interesting and vivid example of unconscious perception that is highly relevant to the disavowal of awareness that could give rise to valid jealousy. A young man, in analysis with Fenichel, had a relationship with a widow considerably older than he. He wished to be free of her but "she held onto him with all her might and occasionally made scenes of jealousy". However, "she anxiously overlooked—as far as was possible—all the indications he gave of his intention to break with her" (p. 94). One morning "after lengthy internal struggles", the young man picked up a girl in the street, chatted and walked with her and sat in the park smoking cigarettes before taking her to a restaurant. In the evening, when undressing, he noticed that he had lost one of his cuff links; he felt annoyed with himself since he had noticed the link was loose when he had been walking in the park. The following day, he visited his older friend and was astonished to see on her hall table a cufflink identical to the one he had lost. His initial reaction was to feel alarmed that the woman had placed it there in order to display her awareness of his sexual adventure the previous day. However, on asking her where she had obtained it, she replied that she had been shopping in an area where she did not usually go and had discovered a park; on resting on a bench she had noticed the cuff link on the ground. He asked what time this had been and she told him one o'clock, which was in fact around the time he had been there with the girl. However, it was apparent that the woman had no conscious awareness that the cuff link was his.

Fenichel comments on the unconscious contribution of both parties:

> Throughout the time he spent in the park, the patient had a bad conscience about his unfaithfulness, and thought of what his friend would say if she saw him there; his whole psychological situation was such as to lend itself to an unconscious betrayal. Furthermore, just before he sat down on the bench he had noticed the open cuff link, and had thus offered his unconscious, as it were, a convenient occasion for a self-betrayal. As for the woman, it is striking, first that

she should pick up the link and take it home, and then that she should put it down in an unusual place so that her friend would see it on entering and would be reminded of his misdemeanour. If she had seen him with the girl and had wanted to confront him with a *corpus delicti*, she could not have done better. These circumstances admit of only one explanation. The only part which chance played in the business was that both of them had come at the same time to the park which was unknown to them before. All the rest was unconscious purposive action at lightening speed. The man sitting on the bench saw the woman nearing; without being in the least aware of it, he was overcome be a storm of feeling in his doubt whether or not he should reveal himself; he decided not to and left the bench quickly with his companion, but not without fulfilling his self-betraying tendency by shaking his arm so that the loose cuff link dropped down. The woman must also have seen and recognised the man. But she did not *want* to see anything . . ." [p. 95]

Fenichel notes that the patient was initially "very much astonished" by this interpretation, but then remembered a further detail. He and the girl had decided to stay in the park for one more cigarette, but very suddenly, in the middle of the cigarette, he had jumped up and said to the girl that they really must go immediately. Fenichel hypothesized that this was the moment that he had unconsciously caught sight of the woman. He concludes:

Thus not only did the two parties, as though by agreement, immediately repress their having seen each other, since that would have been unpleasant for both; the woman also immediately understood the meaning of the loss of the cuff link and reacted accordingly. Indeed she did exactly what the behaviour of the man secretly challenged her to do. When he jumped up and ran away, but lost his link in so doing, he was saying to her: "You are not to *notice* that I have sat here with a girl; but you are to *know* it!" And that is what she did. [p. 96]

The case of Celine—a frenzy of shame and jealousy

Celine, an attractive and highly intelligent woman in her early twenties, sought psychoanalytic help because of her patterns of tormenting anxiety, jealousy, and depression that were recurrent in her relationships with men. She was from a wealthy French background, but had come to Britain to study, in the hope that a new environment would free her from her anguish. In terms of psychiatric diagnosis she would have been described as having a borderline personality disorder—and this was indeed her view of herself, having read some relevant literature.

From the beginning of the therapy, she displayed pronounced jealousy, as well as overwhelming feelings of shame. She was markedly sexually seductive, openly speaking of her desires to engage the analyst in a sexual relationship—and expressing rage when he declined her offer. She viewed his refusal as a personal rejection, despite his efforts both to maintain and to explain a psychoanalytic stance. Indeed she seemed to view the refusal of a sexual relationship as evidence that the analyst regarded her with contempt and found her disgusting—at such times she appeared infused with feelings of shame and would be tearful. Moreover, she became violently jealous of other patients, whom she fantasized were receiving more or better attention from the analyst. If she saw evidence of the existence of other patients she would fly into a rage, accusing the analyst of favouring these rivals. Often she would demand physical contact with the analyst and express anguish when this was refused. Her desperation about her need for bodily engagement was expressed with vivid clarity when she shouted in one session "Do you want me to cut myself or take my clothes off?". Thus her stance towards the analyst in the early weeks and months was characterized mainly by a combination of rage, sexual overtures, and the seeking of physical contact, all pervaded by shame and jealousy.

Her early associations to these feelings towards the analyst were of memories and family accounts of her mother having often been depressed in the first few years of her life, so that Celine might be left for long periods without stimulation, *without being physically touched or held*, and in unbearable states of boredom. These impressions began to throw some light on her feeling that she must fill the sessions with emotional fireworks of rage and sexuality, otherwise the analyst would be withdrawn from her like her mother. It was also apparent that Celine felt she must always seek excitement—through rage, through sexual pursuits and promiscuity, and through the use of stimulating recreational drugs. Such pursuit of excitement was clearly an attempt to avoid the states of severely dysphoric under-stimulation that may often have been a feature of her childhood.

Celine's experience of childhood appeared to have been pervaded (and invaded) by her parents' sexuality. She reported that her mother had affairs, which Celine found herself drawn into. For example, she recalled intercepting phone calls from one of her mother's lovers and shouting abuse down the line at him. She seemed to describe her parents as either fighting each other, or spending hours together in the bedroom having sex, or as having affairs with other people. There were many indications in Celine's behaviour and communications that she believed people are motivated primarily by sex—and that the only way she could be valued was sexually. Her self-esteem would be high in the early stages of a relationship with a man—when she would feel intoxicated with her sense of her sexual power and desirability. Apart from such times, she was generally inclined to experience herself as worthless and unwanted. Moreover, it would often appear that if she were not evoking sexual desire she felt she did not really exist—basically that she did not exist in the mind of the other.

Brief account of a session

During a session following the ending of a relationship that had become repeatedly physically abusive, Celine described various complicated sexual liaisons. She had started a relationship with a new man. In some states of mind she felt full of love towards him. In other states, she felt full of contempt, with triumphant feelings of rage and pleasure in the idea that she can destroy a man's heart. She talked of having sex with various other people in her boyfriend's house. On hearing the sound of another couple making love in the adjoining bedroom, she was filled with intense jealousy and envy. In retaliation she would endeavour to make her own lovemaking as noisy as possible. She also made a point of inflicting prominent love bites on her boyfriend's neck, with the aim of evoking jealousy in another man in the house. When the analyst commented that she seemed not to be allowing herself any time and mental space to come to terms with the ending of her previous relationship, she replied that she was extremely frightened of what she might feel if she were on her own. She thought she was desperately trying to keep away from feelings of loneliness—and indeed thought she could not bear to be on her own for more than a few minutes.

In further exploration, the analyst clarified the following with her. Her real need was for someone to talk to about how she was feeling—but mostly she felt there was no such person available. She needed a *mental* relationship—to have someone hold her in mind, so that she could also begin to hold her own thoughts and feelings in mind. When she found there was no-one available to provide a mental relationship (such as when she could not come to her psychotherapy session), she resorted to a bodily, sexual relationship. In place of emotional communication she would create a situation in which she was engaged in continual sexual activity, whether in fantasy or actuality. Celine then talked of desires to combine a physical and mental relationship—and also spoke of desires for a physical relationship with a woman. The analyst related these points to what seemed likely to have been her early longings to be held and caressed by her mother and to have her mother's thoughtful attention—such needs now being expressed through the sexual modalities of the adult. Celine agreed with this formulation—and talked again of what she had been told of her mother's post-natal depression. She added that she had noticed that a child of a post-natally depressed friend had grown to be particularly difficult and demanding. Celine spoke of relief that the analyst was able to think about her and offer these ideas.

Sibling rivalry

Often Celine would become preoccupied with her boyfriend's previous girlfriends, fearing that he might turn to one of them again—and often raging at him for his retrospective infidelity (in having had girlfriends before her). Some of her vengeful fantasies were extremely sadistic. For example, she imagined scenarios in which she would force her boyfriend to torture and murder these rivals in front of her—a fantasy which she found intensely erotically exciting. Associations led to thoughts of her younger sister, whom she had quite consciously hated in her childhood, although she was very fond of her as an adult. Celine remarked that she had been extremely jealous as a child, just as she was now extremely jealous as a woman. She spoke of how she could never trust her boyfriend's assurance of his love—and how this somehow related to the intolerable fact of his having had other girlfriends, and therefore he could still potentially be attracted to other women. The analyst commented that she might have experienced any reassurances of love from her parents as lacking in sincerity since they had clearly refused to get rid of the hated rival baby—that they had not assured her that they were so blissfully happy with her that they had no desire for any other child. Celine expressed relief and amusement as such feelings and fantasies were made explicit.

Celine also at times disclosed a very paranoid part of her mind that was continually suspicious of what might be going on in the other person's mind. This would be apparent in the transference, where she might feel the analyst was secretly fed up with her and was planning to end her therapy. However, it would often be very pronounced in relation to her boyfriend. She would on occasion search through his belongings for evidence of his having been unfaithful. Sometimes she would become convinced that he wanted to throw her out on the street and direct his love to a rival woman. Associations led to childhood fantasies that the arrival of her sister meant that she was to be eliminated and replaced by this new one. She recalled her profound suspicion when her parents gave her a soft toy, telling her that it was a present from the baby. Her natural incredulity at the idea of a baby giving her a present left her feeling she could not trust a word her parents said.

Rivalry with mother

A recurrent impression was that during her childhood Celine had felt oppressed by her mother's sexuality and painfully excluded from the sexual relationship between her parents and between her mother and her lovers. This combination of stimulation and exclusion had clearly filled her with rage and envy. As an adult she took pleasure in flaunting her own sexuality and in feeling triumphant over her mother (and the analyst in the transference). For example, during one session she spoke of her exciting and frequent sexual activities with her new boyfriend—and then remarked on how she felt it was possible to tell from people's appearance whether they were having much sex or not, and how she thought her mother was not, and how she perceived her mother as "dried up". She talked with triumphant glee of how she would like to tell her mother about her own wonderfully pleasurable sex life. It became apparent that one of her unconscious motivations behind her feeling that she must have sex very frequently was to have more sex than her parents—and in that way to undo her painful sense of childhood exclusion and deprivation. As she left this particular session, she remarked humorously that she was going home now to have sex—thus playfully placing the analyst in the position of the one who is enviously left out and deprived.

A sexual fantasy of triumph over mother

Celine described a sexual fantasy which she had insisted her boyfriend enact with her. In the fantasy he was her mother's lover and she was aged about 11; he confessed to her (in the fantasy) that he was really interested in *her* and had become her mother's lover only in order to be close to Celine; he had intercourse with her and she imagined the physical experience of an 11-year-old girl having sex with a mature man. Celine found this fantasy enactment intensely sexually exciting. She had not thought of the fantasy before and had certainly never enacted it. Such events had never happened in reality with her mother's lover—of that she had no doubt. However, what had happened was that her mother had become so preoccupied with her lover that she had neglected Celine emotionally, just as she was entering puberty. At this time her father too had embarked on an affair. When this was discussed in her therapy, Celine had no difficulty in seeing that her fantasy represented a childhood wish—a triumphant reversal of her actual experience of being humiliatingly abandoned by her mother in favour of her lover. In the fantasy she robbed her mother of her lover.

Bisexuality

At one point, when Celine was speaking of her overwhelming jealousy and rage about her boyfriend's previous girlfriends, the analyst began to wonder whether this might be an expression of her struggles with her own homosexual longings—that she was in a rage at her boyfriend because of envy that he had intimacy with women whilst she did not. In response, Celine acknowledged very strong and persisting longings for physical and emotional intimacy with women. It became clear that when she was in an intimate relationship with a man, the homosexual part of her felt very neglected and left out. Moreover, it became possible to understand how, although she valued relationships with men, including that with her analyst, these left her chronically frustrated and disappointed because the men were not women. She spoke of feeling that men cannot understand women. On the other hand, she felt that a homosexual woman would not be interested in her. These feelings could be linked with her early experiences with her depressed and withdrawn mother—her original feeling that the first woman in her life had not been interested in her. Celine began to see that her tendency to be compulsively promiscuous was in part an expression of her frustrated wish for intimacy with a woman—an amplification of her heterosexuality as a defence against her homosexuality. Moreover, she could understand that her jealous preoccupations with her boyfriend's previous girlfriends and her continual thoughts that he might be unfaithful to her were to some extent a reflection of her projections of her own homosexual wishes. Thus her bisexuality created a triangle of jealousy— whichever polarity of her sexuality was being satisfied, the other polarity would feel excluded and deprived.

Biological features

Biological aspects of Celine's sexuality also became apparent eventually. It became clear that her times of greatest temptation towards promiscuity occurred when she was ovulating and therefore most likely to become pregnant if contraception were not used. In fact, she reported that she had found herself at such times wanting to beg the man not to use a condom—behaviour which was at odds with her conscious desire to avoid pregnancy. Her promiscuity and impulse to place herself in danger of becoming pregnant would, however, be consistent with evolved tendencies for a female to seek sperm from other sexually desirable males whilst maintaining her regular relationship—the "mixed mating strategy" described by Buss (2000). Another feature of her reactions that could be viewed as congruent with a Darwinian perspective was her tendency to become particularly incensed by the thought of her boyfriend having had sexual involvements with women of a different racial group; she did not mind so much the thought that he had been with other women of similar southern European looks like her own. This could be seen as reflecting a kind of loyalty to her own racial (genetic) group—and a fear of other genes being favoured.

Comment

Celine demonstrated many of the features of jealousy described in earlier psychoanalytic writings: projection of her own heterosexual and homosexual impulses, the roots of jealousy in her childhood feelings of exclusion and deprivation (in the Oedipal situations, in relation to her younger sister, and in relation to the parents' lovers), and the wish to rob or triumph over her mother. Celine was continually attempting, unconsciously, to reverse and triumph over her painful childhood feelings of being excluded and unwanted. She would be either the one who *creates* jealousy in the other (through her promiscuity) or the one who *suffers* the agony of jealousy and feelings of exclusion. It was also apparent how sexuality (and the evoking of sexual desire in the other) can incorporate the expression of many desires and needs that are not essentially sexual—such as the wish for physical contact and the wish to matter to another person and to have a place in his or her mind.

Summary

Jealousy is a violent and potentially dangerous passion. It is found in all cultures. Attempts to eliminate it have failed. Pop psychology portrayals of jealousy as reflecting immature insecurity seem naïve. Evolutionary psychology explains how jealousy must be a behavioural response selected by evolutionary pressures, and therefore must serve an adaptive function that relates in some way to the reproduction of an individual's genes. From this perspective, jealousy appears to function as a partial safeguard against sexual treachery and deception. Women tend to be more jealous of the possibility of emotional infidelity, whereas men react much more strongly to the idea of their partner having sex with another man. This marked gender difference is probably because of the danger that, for the man, an unfaithful female partner means that he runs the risk of unknowingly caring for offspring that do not carry his genes. By contrast, the woman does not suffer any reproductive disadvantage if her man has sex with another woman, but she does risk losing his care and protection of her and her children if his emotional attachment shifts to a rival.

There are conflicts and anxieties inherent in the interplay of male and female reproductive strategies. Both men and women may have evolved tendencies to be unfaithful, because of potential reproductive advantages in doing so, and both may also have developed capacities to detect deception. Evolutionary selection has provided the deep structuring of human behaviours and motivations, in order to facilitate the transmission of genes, but these causes are distal and not available to introspection.

Evolutionary theory and psychoanalysis can be viewed as complementary—the former describing the development of the species and the latter the development of the individual. Both lay emphasis upon sexuality as a fundamental force behind human motivations—and both see jealousy as inherent in the human condition. Psychoanalysis exposes the more proximal emotions, impulses, anxieties, and conflicts that drive human beings—and the mechanisms of defence that are commonly used to manage painful or frightening feelings and impulses. Freud described various forms of jealousy rooted in the childhood Oedipus complex, and in rivalry with siblings—and also jealousy that can arise from projection onto the partner of either heterosexual or homosexual impulses to be unfaithful. Riviere and Fenichel described clinical cases which showed deeper roots of jealousy in early feelings of deprivation and wishes to rob the mother. Melanie Klein made a major contribution to understanding how jealousy can grow out of early feelings of greed and envy. Direct observation of children can readily reveal jealousy, from a very early age. Various distinctions have been made between jealousy and envy—mainly based around the point that jealousy involves three people, whereas envy, essentially, does not. Quite often feelings of jealousy may be valid reactions based on accurate perceptions or intuitions—but if these are denied by the partner, the jealous person may conclude that he or she is suffering from irrational feelings or even a delusion.

Notes

1. The field of evolutionary psychology has been criticized by some—for example, Rose and Rose (2000). Certainly it should not be assumed that an evolutionary perspective necessarily invalidates or marginalizes other frameworks, such as the sociological—nor that the inherent plasticity of human behaviour can be ignored.

2. Studies of the incidence of paternal discrepancy indicate a surprisingly high incidence of children having genetic fathers who are different from those who believe they are the father. Baker and Bellis (1995) averaged a number of studies across Europe, Africa, North America, and Oceania, to give an estimate of 9%. Buss (2000) reports the case of a medical researcher who conducted a large scale study of the genetics of breast cancer, which involved DNA fingerprinting of parents and their children; she found a paternal discrepancy rate of 10%, but was afraid to publish this finding for fear of jeopardizing her funding!

3. In a extensive study, several thousand married women were asked to record their sexual desires every day for a period of twenty-four-months, by placing a cross on a chart each day that they experienced sexual desire. Basal body temperature was used as a measure of the phase of the menstrual cycle. The peak of sexual desire coincided with the point of maximum fertility—and women were five times more likely to experience sexual desire when they were ovulating than when they were not.

4. Evolutionary psychologists do not intend that their perspective be viewed as a justification or "excuse" for abusive human behaviour. Rather, it is hoped that an understanding of how behavioural responses may have been selected by evolution can help in modifying or containing these when they are disapproved of by society.

5. The formulations of Riviere and Fenichel were also supported by a later paper by Pao (1969).

6. Melanie Klein's (1957) theory of envy suggests that each gender may envy the attributes of the other. The mother's life-giving breasts and her capacity to create babies inside may be a particular focus of envy—as can the intercourse of the parents. A child's wish to have these capacities and functions (to have the penis, the breasts, or the capacity to bear children) coupled with an awareness of not having these, can engender deep feelings of inadequacy and shame.

CHAPTER FIVE

Shame in the psychoanalytic
consulting room

"As with panic anxiety, most patients prefer to flee from
shame rather than face it. To confront shame therefore
requires a leap of faith on the part of the patient that they will
not be abandoned by the analyst and will be able to tolerate
the pain of the underlying affect"

Bronheim, 1998, p. 83

S hame and the threat of shame are pervasive features of
human life. We are social beings, concerned with finding a
place of recognition, approval and value in the complex
society that human beings have created. If we fail to find such a
place, there is nowhere else to go. Without a positive place in
society, we must identify with the marginalized, the outcasts, the
scape-goats—or else inhabit a no-place of psychosis. From the
beginning of our lives, we strive to be understood, to be loved and
to love. As adults, we need to make our contribution to the social
world, through work, through mating, and through the protection
and raising of the next generation. If we fail in any of these areas, we
feel shame. There is much that can go wrong—many ways in which

to feel defective, inadequate, incompetent, unacceptable, unlovable, and an outcast. Moreover, it is not only our own failings that can lead to shame. Others may force us to feel shame through their ridicule and humiliating criticism—or through overt hostility and abuse. We may as children have been given the message not only that an aspect of our behaviour was unacceptable, but that our very being was bad and defective. Even when the creation of shame was not the intention, we can feel this through the failures of connection and empathic attunement in our childhood interactions with parents or other care-givers.

People who seek the help of analysts or psychotherapists will be riddled with experiences of shame—of one kind or another. This does not mean they will necessarily be aware of such feelings, for shame in its nature tends to be hidden. Shame is a source of shame—and what is shameful is concealed. Signals of shame may be consistently ignored (Harder, 1984), perhaps resulting in the personality style of the "thick skinned" narcissists described by Rosenfeld (1987) and Bateman (1998)—or the "oblivious" (as opposed to "hypervigilant") narcissists described by Gabbard (1996). Thus, many patients (perhaps particularly those with border-line personality disorders) may present, somewhat confusingly, with a mixture of excessive shame and a tendency to ignore appropriate signals of shame—with the result that in their general life they recurrently behave in ways that evoke feelings of shame, without an understanding of how and why this occurs. Hypervigilance to issues of status and comparison with others may combine with a deficiency in the capacity to attend to signals of violating social norms. Such people may be extremely prone to experience shame and rage, and yet also may behave seemingly shamelessly and in ways that shame others. In responding to such a presentation it would be easy to compound their experience of shame.

The core of shame and vulnerability in narcissistically disturbed patients may be covered by layers of protective strategies and organizations—such as the "psychic retreats" described by John Steiner (1993a, 2000, 2002). These may be sufficiently successful much of the time so that the person is not really aware of the extent of their potential feelings of shame. A mental structure character-ized by arrogance, feelings of superiority, and contempt—or the "grandiose self" described by Kernberg (1975), consisting of a fusion of the images of ideal other, ideal self, and actual self—may ward off the real vulnerability and shame, awareness of which may be feared unconsciously as threatening a catastrophe. However, the entry into analysis or therapy will be feared as a potential path to just such a catastrophe. The very fact of seeking help can be felt as a shameful admission of inadequacy.

It is important to recognize that severe shame experienced in childhood is indeed a catastrophe—a psychic devastation—and to return there would be felt to involve a descent into madness and annihilation. If, despite this unconscious dread, the patient does bring his or her vulnerable and fragile self, then the responsibility given to the analyst/therapist is awesome. The responsibility is to provide a safe environment in which the early turmoils of shame can be revisited and worked through—but also, crucially, to avoid actively reshaming the patient. The latter can be extremely difficult in the face of the provocation of being made to suffer some partial elements of the patient's toxic experiences through projective identification and other interpersonal manoeuvres.

The shame threats perceived, consciously or unconsciously, in the psychoanalytic situation are various: the acknowledgment of need and vulnerability (especially by a man, and perhaps particularly in relation to a male analyst—for reasons now given explanation by evolutionary psychology[1]) might be experienced as a shameful "one-down" position (Harder, 1990); the inability to understand one's own mind and the idea that some of one's own communications are unconscious may similarly seem humiliating; the analyst might fail to understand what the patient attempts to describe of his or her experience; the analyst might view the patient as weird—a fear associated with feeling different and not fully human; the analyst might mock or criticize the patient, recreating the shaming scenarios of childhood; the analyst might laugh at the patient—either overtly or in private; the analyst might not like the patient; the patient might fail to interest the analyst; the patient might not be competent as a patient—e.g. might not be able to communicate properly or follow the implicit rules of the analysis; there might be any number of potential misperceptions and failures of mutual understanding between analyst and patient (perhaps partly due to differences of background, nationality or culture).

There are some features of the psychoanalytic situation that act to minimize shame. For example, the use of the couch, which avoids facial contact between patient and analyst, is a brilliant device for helping the patient to feel more free in exploring and communicating their most private inner thoughts, feelings, and fantasies— precisely the aspects of one's mind that are normally concealed. It is well known that Freud claimed to have invented the couch procedure because he did not like to be stared at by his patients all day long. Thus the analyst's feelings of shame are also minimized, despite the discussion of material that would, in any other situation, normally evoke shame. The regularity of the psychoanalytic setting and its peculiarity, as well as the avoidance of ordinary social conversation, all serve to distinguish it as a special place in which the normal contexts of shame do not apply.

On the other hand, there are aspects of the psychoanalytic setting and encounter that can, if not managed sensitively, significantly evoke shame and thereby impede and distort the therapeutic process. First of all, the patient may not know what to expect when visiting an analyst for the first time. This means that he or she does not know what behaviour is appropriate to the situation. There is a tendency in psychoanalytic circles to regard the search for cues regarding expected behaviour as somehow pathological—an expression of a "false self", or a chameleon-like "as if" personality. Perhaps in an extreme form it is, but it is also a normal and necessary part of social intercourse. A stance adopted by many analysts, on seeing a patient for the first time, is one of giving minimal cues as to what he or she might speak of, and simply waiting expectantly. In addition, visual facial cues may be restricted. The rationale for this is that it allows the patient's concerns and anxieties to emerge more clearly, with minimal shaping by the analyst. This may be true to some extent, but the stance is abnormal in terms of how human beings behave towards each other in most other situations. The patient is deprived of normally expected cues and therefore he or she will be reacting to an abnormal situation—one which is maximally likely to evoke shame and social anxiety. Moreover, the patient's communicative initiatives are not met with the facial, verbal, and body language responses that he or she would normally elicit when talking to another person and which usually communicate reciprocally messages of acceptance, understanding and empathy. It is somewhat like the "still face" experiments (Tronick *et al.*, 1978) where the baby withdraws because his or her communicative initiative is met with an unwelcoming response.

The restricted social and personal cues offered by the analyst, combine with an expectation that the patient reveal a great deal of extremely personal and perhaps inherently shame-related information. Many patients will not protest about this, partly because the issues are difficult to identify and articulate, and also because the position the patient is in is shameful—and therefore will be concealed. Some time ago, an unusually assertive and articulate patient explained the problem to me. She protested that I was behaving in a very strange way, not giving her feedback, showing little body language, not responding to her humour, and so on. How did I expect her to be *open* and to talk to me about her inner feelings and thoughts when I was so *closed*, concealing so much of myself? She was pointing out that the distribution within the shame economy was profoundly asymmetrical! Fortunately, because she presented her experience of me and of my way of behaving so clearly, we were able to explore the anxieties that lay behind it. We were able to understand, for example, that she normally relied on her conversational and interactional skills, including her capacities to flirt, as a means of providing her with a sense of control—this being very important to her in the context of a childhood characterized by chaos. Her inability to experience her familiar sense of control when talking to me gave rise to a quiet, but mounting, feeling of panic—the anxiety of disrupted expectations. Moreover, we saw that my lack of a conventional interactional response to her led her to feel that I did not like her, was not interested in her, and did not care about her. Her anxieties were all in the area of shame and shame-anxiety. Eventually she did disclose an extremely shame-laden, vulnerable, and hidden core of her personality. One might say that this capacity to reveal latent underlying anxieties is precisely the value of the "neutral" psychoanalytic stance. This is true—but only if the issues become sufficiently apparent to be addressed. The patient had been thinking of breaking off her therapy because of her distress—and the nature of this had not been apparent to me until she forcibly and rather courageously brought it to my attention. A less assertive patient might simply have left without indicating clearly why. It is important to recognize that the psychoanalytic stance and style may sometimes create considerable shame-anxiety because of the deprivation of normal visual, verbal, and body-language cues.

A second potential source of shame in the psychoanalytic situation can lie in the experience of the analyst's interpretation. If this is perceived as a quasi-oracular pronouncement which reframes the patient's communications in terms of meanings that were not in any way consciously intended, then inevitably shame will result. This is because the *expected* understanding of the communication is absent. In place of an empathic response there is substituted quite a different meaning. For some, narcissistically vulnerable, patients, this bypassing of the empathic response (the understanding from within their own frame of reference) may be intolerable—even if the interpretation is recognized as essentially correct in certain respects. Rosenfeld (1987) recognized that sometimes such a scenario can lead to impasse. Steiner's (1993b) discussion of patient-centred and analyst-centred interpretations may also relate to this problem.

Some of Heinz Kohut's examples

Kohut's writings contain many examples of patients who could tolerate analysis only if particular emphasis was placed upon empathy in the framing of the analyst's comments. Any deviation from the patient's own perspective would be experienced as psychologically annihilating. Such patients are profoundly shame-prone and extremely sensitive to the *manner* in which the analyst speaks to them

The hobby

One of Kohut's examples (1996) concerned a patient who had a hobby which his previous analyst had apparently belittled because he spent so much time and money on it and had lost several jobs as a result. Eventually the man's shame about the hobby had diminished sufficiently that he was able to speak to Kohut about it. He talked of what it meant to him, how enjoyable it was, and so on. Kohut listened for about 40 minutes, speaking only when the patient asked if he understood some technical detail. Then Kohut asked when the hobby had started. The patient told him, but was then silent for the rest of the session and for many sessions afterwards. Kohut's later understanding of this sequence was that the patient had reached a point where he could attempt to share his interest and excitement with the analyst, hoping for a mirroring response of interest in return—but after 40 minutes or so, Kohut had felt compelled to be "an analyst" by inquiring about the origin of the hobby. The implicit message of his simple enquiry (not even an interpretation) was that the patient should undertake analytic work rather than enjoy talking about the hobby—and the patient's response was to withdraw, in shame and anger, for a considerable time.

Tone of voice

In another example, Kohut described the reactions of a severely disturbed man when he announced that he would be away for a week. The patient shifted to a near delusional grandiose and paranoid state of mind in response. Kohut attempted a variety of interpretations of the meaning of his announcement, but none made any difference until he stumbled upon the crucial point that it had apparently been his tone of voice that had provoked the patient's withdrawal and regression. The patient had experienced this as unempathic and defensive—and Kohut recognized that the patient had been correct in his perception of this since he had indeed feared a stormy response to his announcement. After this sequence had been explored and interpreted, the patient returned to a less disturbed state of mind.

The dream of the fish

In a third example, Kohut (1971) described a more healthy patient, at a later stage of analysis, who brought some diaries to a session and read them to the analyst. Following this, the patient had a two part dream:

> he had been fishing and had caught a big fish which he proudly brought to his father; however, the father was not admiring but was critical; in the second part, he saw Christ on the cross, suddenly slumping, his muscles relaxing as he died.

From this reaction, expressed through the dream, Kohut deduced that the patient must have detected some lack of enthusiasm on the analyst's part when he brought the diaries and had reacted with shame. He thought it was quite likely that he, the analyst, may have indeed perceived the reading of the diaries as an impediment to the more direct and spontaneous production of analytic material. On reflection, he thought he may not fully have appreciated the emotional meaning of the patient's bringing of the diaries, that had not been a resistance to analysis but an analytic gift—like the fish in the dream. Therefore he concluded that the dream illustrated how the patient's mood had slumped in response—he had felt deflated, and had resorted to a masochistic merger fantasy represented by the dream's allusion to the biblical account of Christ's reunion with God the Father. The childhood background provided a further context for the patient's response. His father had tended to be self-preoccupied and had responded negatively and critically to the child's progress in whatever area—just like the father in the dream.

A critical patient

A further example (Kohut, 1984) concerns a patient who had seen a number of analysts and therapists prior to approaching Kohut. He was extremely critical of all of them, describing them as completely lacking in empathy. He was also very critical of his parents—describing his mother as having been totally involved with her church and its dogma, whilst his father had been withdrawn and uninvolved with the patient as a child. The presenting problem was a chronic feeling of unreality.

Kohut was somewhat uneasy about taking on this patient, particularly in view of his relentless criticism of previous analysts and the possibility of an underlying paranoid psychosis. Despite this reservation, they did proceed to work together and the patient established an essentially positive attitude towards the analyst and seemed accepting of many of Kohut's interpretations. However, an alarming deterioration took place after about a year, following Kohut's being away for several weeks. The patient became dominated by headaches and could talk of little else. Moreover, the quality of these evolved from a more ordinary physical pain to a kind of unspeakable discomfort that seemed more psychological than physical. Kohut tried to link the patient's headaches to the break in the analysis, interpreting feelings of abandonment, loss of support, and anger. The patient did not find these interpretations helpful, pointing out that he had not felt upset when Kohut had been away, nor initially on his return. Then some further material suggested another interpretive possibility. Kohut put to the patient that perhaps as a result of analytic work the patient had become more open to emotional interactions with the world and that as a consequence he was now facing anxieties and tensions from which previously he had walled himself off; this development was leaving him continually traumatized and overburdened by emotional impingements. The patient reacted favourably to this interpretation, providing further confirmatory material and generally appearing much brighter and more cheerful. However, after a few sessions exploring this theme, the patient began to criticize Kohut severely, accusing him of lacking all understanding and of ruining him. He also complained of people in his environment who were upsetting him with their behaviour or manner.

Kohut comments in his account of this analysis that the patient's complaints about him were always based around real flaws in his emotional response, even if these were exaggerated. Eventually some understanding of the patient's experience of Kohut began to emerge. Apparently he had felt that Kohut's interpretations, both about the break and about his sense of impingement, had been correct—but he had experienced them as intellectually generated rather than being based in a true empathy with what he felt. The impression that Kohut had presented ideas from his own point of view, rather than working from the patient's point of view, had repeated aspects of the trauma of his early life with his self-preoccupied parents. Kohut notes:

> The patient, as I finally grasped, insisted—and had a right to insist—that I learn to see things exclusively in his way and not at all in my way. [1984, p. 182]

As Kohut's stance altered along these lines, the patient presented further material throwing new light on the paternal transference. His reproaches became more focused. Specifically he complained that both Kohut and his father had wanted him to look up to them rather than responding to his own ideas and initiatives.

Thus, in this case and in the other examples, a patient is described whose childhood background had been characterized by a lack of responsiveness to, or active discouragement of, his own initiatives. These rage and shame promoting circumstances were then repeated in the transference experience and interaction with the analyst. Kohut describes how he had to adapt to the patient's need to have his or her own point of view given privilege over the analyst's point of view. He comments:

> To hammer away at the analysand's transference distortions brings no results; it only confirms the analysand's conviction that the analyst is as dogmatic, as utterly sure of himself, as walled off in the self-righteousness of a distorted view as the pathogenic parents ... had been. Only the analyst's continuing sincere acceptance of the patient's reproaches as (psychologically realistic), followed by a prolonged (and ultimately successful) attempt to look into himself and remove the inner barriers that stand in the way of his empathic grasp of the patient, ultimately have a chance to turn the tide. [1984, p. 182]

By the analyst's being willing to accept and thereby validate the patient's experience and point of view, the analysis became able to move on towards a deeper understanding of the transference.

Shame in the transference

If shame has been a particular feature of the patient's childhood experience, then inevitably there will be shame in the transference. Both patient and analyst will experience it. Even if the emphasis is mostly upon the *patient's* sense of shame, or fear of shame, there will be moments when the tables are turned and the *analyst* is made to experience shame (in the form of feeling exposed, criticized, and revealed to be inadequate). A shame-prone patient may often have an accurate perception of real areas of narcissistic vulnerability in the analyst and these will be exploited in order to inflict shame. The analyst might endeavour to adopt an empathic stance and to avoid shaming the patient. To begin with this may seem to lead to a favourable response in shame-prone patients. Kohut notes that sometimes an initial positive development is then followed by an alarming deterioration, with a barrage of criticism against the analyst. He asks why there is this initial period of calm before a storm—and answers as follows:

> What happens is nothing else but the transference clicking into place. Thus during the calm before the storm, the analyst and the patient have jointly explored the patient's traumatic past, allied in the shared pursuit of a goal; once the storm breaks loose, however, the analytic situation has become the traumatic past and the analyst has become the traumatising selfobject of early life. [1984, p. 178]

Minimization of shame in the consulting room

Although shame is inevitable in the transference, if shame has been a feature of the patient's childhood background, it is important to try to minimize shame in the non-transference aspects of the relationship. Without a non-transference area existing alongside the transference, we would have a transference *psychosis* in which the "as if" nature is lost and the analyst is perceived as being really like the shaming figures of childhood. This may indeed be what happens sometimes in the states of impasse that can arise with shame-prone patients.

What complicates the situation is that the underlying shame and fear of shame may not be obvious (Retzinger, 1998). Instead the patient's presentation may be one of aloof withdrawal, arrogance, concealment, hostility—and a generally rather obscure mode of communication. This is because shame is hidden. Shame is shameful! It is never expressed overtly and directly. Patients simply do not come along to an analyst or therapist saying "my problem is that I suffer from excessive shame". By contrast, patients might quite easily say that they suffer from excessive guilt, since that is much less shameful. Because the shame is hidden, the analyst may be drawn to respond to other more overt aspects of the presentation, especially the apparent hostility. This can then lead to an interpretive stance that is shaming—even though this would not be the analyst's intention. Narcissistic rage may then be provoked. This may further conceal the underlying shame—and may lead to interpretive foci that are experienced as humiliating and evoke more shame. In such a way, an impasse can develop. Lewis (1971), in studying many transcripts of psychotherapeutic sessions, found that unidentified and unanalysed shame was very often the basis of negative therapeutic reactions and impasse.

Rosenfeld (1987) describes this problem in relation to what he calls "thin skinned narcissists" who are shame prone:

> They are hypersensitive and easily hurt in everyday life and analysis. Moreover, when the sensitive narcissistic patient is treated in analysis as if he is the "thick-skinned" patient he will be severely traumatised. The analysis and the patient may be brought near to collapse, especially if the destructive aspects of a patient's behaviour are constantly repeated in the analyst's interpretations. Such patients can end the analysis very much worse off than before. In my experience the "thin-skinned" narcissistic patients were, as children, repeatedly severely traumatised in their feelings of self-regard. They seem to have felt persistently and excessively inferior, ashamed and vulnerable, and rejected by everybody. ... such traumatised and vulnerable people find it very difficult to cope with any trauma or failure. However, one has to be particularly on guard not to add to these traumas by making mistakes in our analytic approach which humiliate such people and put them down. These mistakes are very difficult to remedy afterwards. [pp. 274–275]

However, it is not easy to avoid shaming certain patients. Although a cold and distant analytic stance can be experienced as discouraging to communication of shameful areas because of the threat of further shame, an ostensibly friendly and supportive style can be experienced as patronizing. The emergence of vulnerability in a patient who has hidden within some kind of psychic retreat (Steiner, 1993), perhaps behind a façade of arrogance, can be potentially humiliating and that person may be extremely sensitive to the quality of the analyst's response. It really is a matter of using a sense of tact to determine what kind of stance from the analyst is most tolerable and helpful to the particular patient. What may be unhelpful is a stance that privileges the communication of "truth" regardless of how this is experienced by the patient.

In my own efforts to avoid evoking unnecessary shame in the consulting room, I have found certain styles of speaking to the patient to be helpful. First, I try to acknowledge and perhaps articulate the patient's experience from an empathic position. Then, in making interpretations that go beyond the empathic surface, I try to indicate how my idea about what is going on derives from the patient's own communications. In this way, my stance is one of trying to understand more of what the patient is trying to tell me, consciously and unconsciously—rather than appearing to present a view of my own. This is perhaps somewhat along the lines of the stance of "learning from the patient", discussed by Casement (1985, 1990, 2002). I also try to make my own thought processes explicit so that the patient can follow my reasoning and inferences. In these ways I try to avoid appearing like an oracular authority making interpretive pronouncements, but instead endeavour to convey a sense that I am a fellow human being struggling to use my specialist knowledge to understand the patient and to share this understanding with him/her. Finally I try to behave in as "normal" a way as possible while maintaining an analytic stance—giving ordinary vocalizations of understanding, encouragement, and emotional response occasionally (i.e. noises that are not necessarily words), and some facial response if the patient is sitting up rather than lying on the couch. However, I obviously do not always succeed in this, as evidenced by the comments of the patient I described above.

There is one area in which I take a view which may be at odds with that of some other analysts. I think that while transference interpretations, about the patient's unconscious conflicts in relation to the analyst, are extremely important, they should be used sparingly. This is because too much attention to the transference can evoke inhibiting shame and can undermine the patient's own efforts at autonomous strivings for understanding. If most of the analyst's comments relate to the patient's relationship with the analyst—and particularly if much of what the patient says is reformulated as unconsciously referring to that relationship—the patient may come to feel self-conscious about speaking, wondering what the analyst is going to make of it. Again this relates to the shift of the locus of meaning from the patient's frame of reference to that of the analyst. Another aspect of this is that if every communication is taken as unconsciously a transference communication—with the implication that this is the most important aspect—then the patient's own autonomous strivings after understanding may be invalidated, resulting in a pattern of chronic undetected shame pervading the analysis. Sometimes patients may have valid insights into their own motivations and preoccupations; and sometimes may be engaging in important analytic work through thinking and exploring their own thoughts, feelings, and fantasies, without the need for anything from the analyst other than his or her attention and reverie. To impose an interpretation or other analytic activity when none is required can be like a parent unnecessarily interfering with a child's exploration and practice at a new skill—an interference that would tend to evoke shame and rage. This rage would not be an expression of "envy" of the skills of the parent or analyst, but of frustration at the blocking of strivings after autonomy. The analytic function—of being able to discern and think about communications from the unconscious—is a learnable skill which patients will indeed learn and carry out if allowed to do so. When the patient is actively exploring in this way, there may be no need for the analyst to say very much at all during a session—a style of work that would contrast with the rather active approach favoured by many analysts today, but one which might be congruent with a more classical approach.

One of Kohut's examples described above concerned a patient who brought some old diaries to the session and proceeded to read them aloud to the analyst. Kohut acknowledged that, as "analyst", he may have felt slightly uneasy about this deviation from more direct and spontaneous communication, but nevertheless believed the bringing of the diaries was an important analytic "gift" and was useful to the process of understanding. A colleague told me of a situation many years ago when he was first seeing an analyst. Finding the interaction with the analyst extremely difficult and frustrating, he suddenly felt moved to write an account of his experience with the analyst and his own perception and under-standing of it. The process of writing did indeed release some new insights into what was going on. With some anxiety and shame he took the piece of writing to his analytic session, proposing to read it aloud. The analyst was not dismissive of the writing, but asked if the patient might talk about it rather than reading it. Although the patient complied with this suggestion, he felt that something was lost in not having the opportunity to present the more carefully articulated written account. Probably many analysts would have responded similarly, but I wonder if the insistence on the *spontaneous* interaction may paradoxically inhibit and eclipse other potentially important modes of communication and emotional growth that at times present themselves. What is clear is that the threat of potential shame may inhibit the patient from exploring other ways of being and communicating in the analytic situation—for example, even something as simple as trying a chair rather than the couch.

It may not only be psychoanalytic patients who are inhibited by shame. Psychoanalysts tend to form communities with strong group cohesion, the mutual support being very important since the work is so difficult and unusual. Psychoanalysis, as an occupation, is regarded by most people as rather odd and few outside the profession have much understanding of it. It is not readily comparable to any other activity and way of life. Therefore it is only amongst other analysts that we find empathy and understanding of our work and daily experience. The lack of ready understanding found amongst society generally means that declaring one's occupation and identity as a psychoanalyst may be a source of shame as well as pride. It also means that the acceptance of other analysts is of particular importance—with an inevitable result that deviations from group cultural norms will be exceptionally liable to evoke the threat of shame. The psychoanalytic culture is likely therefore to be particularly conservative.

 gp can help

Shame pervades the psychoanalytic situation. It cannot be eliminated. However, I hope that these few remarks here may help to highlight its significance and facilitate sensitivity to factors that may increase or diminish its presence and power. We may thus more easily discern the vulnerabilities and privacies that lie hidden beneath the patient's social cover and complex layers of defence. Then, in the warmth of recognition by an other, and touched by the healing filaments of empathy, the broken, banished, frozen, and fragile parts—imprisoned in shame—may be released and woven into the fabric of the personality—the human connection restored.

Note

1. A hypothesis prevalent amongst evolutionary psychologists is that men tend to be less inclined than women to express negative emotion because reproductive success involves greater competition between men than between women (e.g. Archer, 1996). Expression of emotional distress between men would, according to this view, tend to be

regarded as a sign of weakness and lead to a loss of status, and therefore a lowering of reproductive attractiveness to women. This would be the "distal" evolutionary explanation of the widely recognized differences in emotional expression between men and women. In more "proximal" psychoanalytical terms, the same tendencies might be experienced as a fear of passivity or homosexuality. Either way, they would be associated with shame.

Concluding summary

I t is possible to summarize the preceding discussion by a few points. For the benefit of the non-specialist reader, I have tried to write these in a simple and clear way, eschewing psycho-analytic terms.

- Many people suffer from crippling feelings of shame (and embarrassment, self-consciousness, and shyness). These are exaggerations of feelings that are quite normal and necessary. By contrast, some other people may fail to recognize appropriate signals of shame—and may behave in ways that are "shame-less".
- Shame pervades human life, but is often hidden. One of its functions is to encourage conformity to the prevailing group and culture. Some people experience rejection by a group because they fail to be sensitive to signals of shame.
- Active shaming, especially in childhood, can be very harmful to a person's self-esteem. Chronic rage can be one result. Wishes to turn the tables and shame others can also be prominent. Severe abuse in childhood can result in *toxic shame*, which can be devastating.

- However, a person may be greatly influenced by feelings of shame even when he or she has not suffered active shaming. This is because shame arises from all manner of failures of connection and understanding between one human being and another. If a child expresses a need, but this is not understood and met empathically, the child will experience shame. The subtlety and pervasiveness of such processes may be part of the reason why shame is often overlooked.

- Repeated experiences in childhood of psychological needs not being recognized, understood empathically, accepted and met, may lead to those needs being concealed. A "false self" may develop—built upon shame—such that an adaptation to the parental expectations hides the more authentic feelings and needs.

- Shame is a powerful inhibitor of honest emotional communication. Some people develop personalities organized around the concealment and *repudiation* of feelings of weakness, neediness, vulnerability, and inadequacy. A façade of strength, confidence—and particularly arrogance—may be presented. In some cases, there may be an internal turning against a part of the mind associated with shame—an inner cruel oppression of the emotionally needy part.

- Shame is about feelings of inadequacy. Whilst feelings of inadequacy can be attached to failures in any human endeavour, the most fundamental sense of inadequacy is social—arising originally in the relationship with the mother.

- The early facial mirroring relationship with the mother is a powerful way in which emotion is transmitted. The mother's smile or lack of it has a direct effect on the chemistry and development of the infant's brain. A face that is not responsive in the way the baby expects is extremely disturbing to the infant—and evokes shame.

- It is the same with adults. A smile will alter the recipient's brain chemistry and induce pleasure.

- The lack of an expected smile is like an encounter with a *stranger*. Indeed the so-called "stranger anxiety", often shown at around eight-months of age, has some of the qualities of a shame reaction. A little later, when children have to come to terms with the relationship between the parents that excludes them—the Oedipus situation and the primal scene—he or she has *become* the stranger and experiences not only shame but also jealousy.

- Childhood rivalries with siblings may also lay down a template for later feelings of jealousy. Perceptions or fantasies of a rival being preferred will give rise to feelings of shame, as well as anger.

- Jealousy is inherent in human behaviour and emotion and cannot be eradicated. It is an inevitable emotional corollary of the need to compete for limited resources, including sexual and reproductive resources (i.e. competition for a mate). Sexual jealousy has probably evolved as a very strongly entrenched strategy for protecting the transmission of one's own genes. This applies particularly to men. Men in general display stronger reactions to situations that might evoke explicitly sexual jealousy—the danger of the partner being impregnated by another man—whilst women show stronger reactions to the prospect of losing the man's love and loyalty.

- The belief that jealousy is a sign of personality flaws, low self-esteem or insecurity, or abnormal wishes to control the partner, can be misleading and harmful, leading to additional and unnecessary feelings of shame. Both men and women have evolved emotional radar for detecting infidelity in their sexual partner. Attempting to deal with jealousy in a relationship by trying to ignore or cognitively minimize such feelings may be, as Buss (2000) notes, like responding to a fire by switching off the smoke alarm.

- Jealousy can, however, certainly be exacerbated by psycho-dynamic factors, especially by unconsciously attributing to the other (projection) the person's own (heterosexual and homo-sexual) impulses to be unfaithful. Unconscious fears of retaliation for early feelings of rivalry and greed towards the mother can also play a part.

- Childhood experiences of abandonment and deception by care-givers can also predispose a person to enhanced reactions of jealousy. Doubts about parental love, perhaps based on accurate perceptions of hostility, ambivalence, and neglect, may mean that in later life the person cannot trust their partner's love and will anticipate rejection, deception, and betrayal.

- The encounter with a psychoanalyst or psychotherapist is fraught with potential shame. Some aspects of the psychoanalytic stance can function to elicit underlying anxiety (and in that respect are useful), but at the same time can evoke shame (which can be inhibiting). There are ways in which the analyst can minimize the potential for unnecessary shame. This is important because patients will communicate only those aspects of their emotions that they expect to be understood and accepted; the rest will simply be concealed and may remain unconscious. Signals of shame tell the patient what is safe and what is not safe to attempt to communicate—but these signals are registered unconsciously.
- Fundamentally, shame is about a broken connection between one human being and others—a breach in the understanding, expectation, and acceptance that is necessary for a sense of being a valued member of the human family. The cure for shame is the empathy provided by an other.

A note on psychoanalysis for the general reader

Since some readers may not be familiar with the theory and practice of psychoanalysis, I have outlined a few brief notes below. These give only a simplified general outline, but it is hoped that they may provide a context which helps to make the rest of the text more accessible.

A developmental view

Psychoanalysis takes a developmental view of the emotional and mental health difficulties of the adult, seeing these as rooted, to a large extent, in the interpersonal experiences between child and parents (or other significant care-givers) in the first few years of life. Later stages are not ignored, since each phase of life poses its own challenges—and adolescence is particularly important—but the earliest years are regarded as the most crucial, since this is the period when the developing brain and personality are at their most vulnerable. This is also the time when the child is building up an internal map or model of the world, including the world of other people and relationships. The expectations of how other people will respond to one's needs are laid down during these first few years and continue to influence our emotions and behaviour for the rest of our life.

Transference

During psychoanalysis (or psychoanalytic psychotherapy), the analyst endeavours to bring to the light of consciousness the patient's (or analysand's) deep wishes, fantasies, and anxieties derived from childhood (and from the child parts within the mind of the adult) and to show how these are influencing the person unconsciously and contributing to difficulties that person is experiencing. An important focus of the exploration is the patient's relationship with the analyst—particularly in its more unconscious aspects. Those features of the relationship that are derived (transferred) from the childhood experiences and from the infantile parts of the adult are called the *"transference"*.

Free association

The patient in analysis is not given any direction or structure regarding what to talk about, other than the request that he or she attempt as far as possible to speak freely of whatever comes to mind. This free-flowing kind of discourse is called *"free association"*. An excellent discussion of this can be found in Bollas, 2002. In practice it is not really possible to speak entirely freely, because the person endeavouring to do so will encounter various anxieties and resistances—such as feelings of shame, fears of the analyst's disapproval, and so on. Much of the analytic work involves understanding these inner resistances.

The unconscious mind

Through the use of free association, and also through attention to dreams, it becomes possible to understand the more *unconscious* parts of the mind. Freud first discerned some of the features of the unconscious mind through his study of dreams. He found that the unconscious mind contains wishes, feelings, fantasies, and perceptions that are repressed from consciousness because they are disturbing. A variety of *defences* are used against awareness of troubling elements of potential awareness. Analytic work involves undoing these defences and thereby expanding the area of consciousness. In addition to containing aspects of emotional life that are repressed from consciousness, the unconscious mind also has its own mode of "thinking" and representing ideas, which is quite different from that of the conscious mind (Mollon, 2001b). Freud described aspects of this mode in his outline of processes employed in generating the images of dreams.

The Oedipus complex

Psychoanalysis is a field with many different points of view and emphasis, as groups of analysts have explored different clinical states using a variety of theoretical frameworks. Freud originally gave particular emphasis to the *Oedipus* complex, wherein the child wishes to be close and special to one parent whilst feeling hostile and rivalrous with the other—giving rise to anxieties about retaliation. In the Oedipal situation, the little boy may fear *castration*—an idea that is sometimes thought of in literal terms and sometimes more metaphorically as a deprivation of power. Little girls may unconsciously fear analogous damage to their own internal organs. The Oedipus complex is still seen as important by most analysts, but many other areas of developmental difficulty and conflict have also been identified. Some analysts, particularly those working in the tradition of Melanie Klein, tend to emphasize difficulties arising from the child's own inherent hostility and fantasy—describing how the small child's angry and hostile fantasies colour and distort his or her perception of the world. Others, such as those developing the *attachment theory* of John Bowlby, emphasize how the child builds up *internal models* of the world based on real interactions and relationships (rather than upon fantasy). Most analysts see the inner world of models of relationships as derived from a *combination* of fantasy and actual experience.

The primal scene

Some analytic theorists place importance on the child's feelings of envy and painful exclusion from the intimate relationship between the parents. The child's encounter with the parents in intercourse (either in reality or in the child's fantasy) is sometimes called the *primal scene*.

Instinct and object

Readers new to psychoanalysis are often puzzled by the use of the term "object" to refer to people with whom one has a relationship. The origin of this convention lies in Freud's conceptualization of the developmental stages of the sexual instinct, or libido. In his original theorizing, he did not really think in terms of relationships but in terms of instinctual satisfaction and frustration. The sexual instinct, during its different phases of development, was seen as having changing aims and objects. Although later psychoanalysts did emphasize relationships, the convention of using the term "object" has persisted.

Narcissism

Although human beings clearly seek relationships with others from the beginning of life, people can also withdraw their love or desire for others and may instead become preoccupied with their own physical or mental self. This is called *narcissism*. It may be associated with grandiosity and exhibitionism—and shame. An American psychoanalyst called Heinz Kohut made an important contribution by suggesting that narcissism is not inherently an unhealthy tendency, but actually has its own line of development from more primitive to more mature forms. For example, crude grandiosity and exhibitionism may develop later into a pleasure in pursuing goals and displaying realistic achievements. When analysts speak of narcissistic vulnerability or narcissistic injury, they are referring to sensitivities in the area of self-esteem and self-image.

Results of psychoanalysis

When analysis works well, the patient will gradually achieve a greater self-knowledge and self-acceptance, so that he or she is less driven by unconscious forces which create frustrating repetitive patterns of emotion and behaviour. This enables an increased inner freedom of thought and choice about how to respond and relate to others. The person's sense of self will have expanded and there will be greater integration of previously repressed or split-off parts of the mind and personality.

REFERENCES

Allen, J. (2001). *Traumatic Relationships and Serious Mental Disorders.* Chichester: Wiley.

Amsterdam, B., & Levitt, M. (1980). Consciousness of self and painful self-consciousness. *Psychoanalytic Study of the Child.*, 35: 67–83.

Archer, J. (1996). Sex differences in social behavior: are the social roles and evolutionary explanations compatible? *American Psychologist,* 51: 909–917.

Arieti, S., & Bemporad, J. (1980). *Severe and Mild Depression.* London: Tavistock.

Bach, S. (1980). Self-love and object-love: some problems of self- and object-constancy, differentiation, and integration. In: R. Lax, S. Bach & J. A. Burland (Eds.), *Rapprochement. The Critical Subphase of Separation–Individuation.* New York: Aronson.

Bailey, K. G. (1987). *Human Paleopsychology. Applications to Aggression and Pathological Processes.* Hillsdale, NJ: Erlbaum.

Baker, J. M., & Bellis, M. (1995). *Human Sperm Competition: Copulation, Masturbation and Infidelity.* London: Chapman Hall.

Barkow, J. H., Cosmides, L., & Tooby, J. (1992). *The Adapted Mind. Evolutionary Psychology and the Generation of Culture.* Oxford: Oxford University Press.

Bateman, A. W. (1998). Thick- and thin-skinned organisations and enactments in borderline and narcissistic disorders. *International Journal of Psychoanalysis*, *79*, 13–26.

Benedict, R. (1946). *The Chrysanthemum and the Sword*. Boston: Houghton Mifflin.

Bhugra, D. (1993). Cross-cultural aspects of jealousy. *International Review of Psychiatry*, *5*: 271–280

Bion, W. R. (1959). Attacks on linking. *International Journal of Psycho-Analysis*, *40*(5–6) [reprinted in *Second Thoughts. Selected Papers on Psycho-Analysis*. London: Maresfield/Karnac].

Birkhead, T. & Moller, A. (Eds.) (1998). *Sperm Competition and Sexual Selection*. New York: Academic Press.

Bollas, C. (2000). *Hysteria*. London: Routledge.

Bollas, C. (2002). *Free Association*. Cambridge: Icon Books.

Bowlby, J. (1980). *Attachment and Loss, Volume 3: Loss, Sadness and Depression*. London: Hogarth.

Bowlby, J. (1991). *Charles Darwin. A New Life*. New York: Norton.

Bronheim, H. E. (1998). *Body and Soul. The Role of Object Relations in Faith, Shame and Healing*. Northvale, NJ: Aronson.

Broucek, F. (1979). Efficacy in infancy: a review of some experimental studies and their possible implications for clinical theory. *International Journal of Psychoanalysis*, *60*: 311–316.

Broucek, F. (1982). Shame and its relation to early narcissistic developments. *International Journal of Psychoanalysis*, *63*: 369–378.

Broucek, F. (1991). *Shame and the Self*. New York: Guilford.

Buunk, B. P., Angleitner, A., Oubaid, V., & Buss, D. M. (1996). Sex differences in jealousy in evolutionary and cultural perspective: tests from the Netherlands, Germany, and the United States. *Psychological Science*, *7*: 359–363.

Buss, A. H. (1980). *Self-consciousness and Social Anxiety*. San Francisco: W. H. Freeman.

Buss, D. M. (1999). *Evolutionary Psychology. The New Science of the Mind*. New York: Oxford University Press.

Buss, D. M. (2000). *The Dangerous Passion. Why Jealousy is as Necessary as Love and Sex*. London: Bloomsbury.

Buss, D. M., Larsen, R. J., Westen, D., & Semmelroth, J. (1992). Sex differences in jealousy: evolution, physiology, and psychology. *Psychological Science*, *3*(4): 251–255.

Casement, P. (1985). *On Learning from the Patient*. London: Routledge.

Casement, P. (1990). *Further Learning from the Patient*. London: Routledge.

Casement, P. (2002). *Learning from our Mistakes*. London: Routledge.

Clanton, G., & Smith, L. G. (Eds.) (1998). *Jealousy*. Lanham, Maryland: University Press of America.

Cohen, M. B., Baker, G., Cohen, R. A., Fromm-Reichmann, F., & Weigert, E. V. (1954). An intensive study of twelve cases of manic-depressive psychosis. *Psychiatry, 17*: 103–137.

Concoran, R. (2000). "Theory of mind" in other clinical conditions; is selective "theory of mind" deficit exclusive to autism? In: S. B. Cohen (Ed.), *Understanding Other Minds. Perspectives from Developmental Cognitive Neuroscience* (2nd edn). Oxford: Oxford University Press.

Darwin, C. R. (1872). *The Expression of Emotions in Man and Animals*. Chicago: University of Chicago Press.

De Paola, H. (2001). Panel Report. Envy, jealousy and shame. *International Journal of Psychoanalysis, 82*: 381–384.

Ellis, A. (1988). Rational and irrational jealousy. In: G. Clanton & L. G. Smith (Eds.), *Jealousy*. Lanham, Maryland: University Press of America.

Erikson, E. H. (1950). *Childhood and Society*. New York: Norton.

Fairbairn, W. R. D. (1952). *Psychoanalytic Studies of the Personality*. London: Routledge.

Fenichel, O. (1926). Concerning unconscious communication. Reprinted in *The Collected Papers of Otto Fenichel. First Series*. Norton: New York, 1953.

Fenichel, O. (1935). A contribution to the psychology of jealousy. *Imago, 21*: 143–157 [reprinted in *The Collected Papers of Otto Fenichel. First Series*. Norton: New York, 1953].

Fenichel, O. (1946). *The Psychoanalytic Theory of Neurosis*. London: Routledge.

Fonagy, P., Gergely, G., Jurist, E. L., & Target, M. (2002). *Affect Regulation, Mentalisation, and the Development of the Self*. New York: Other Press.

Freud, A. (1966). *The Ego and the Mechanisms of Defence*. London: Hogarth.

Freud, S. (1901). The psychopathology of everyday life. *Standard Edition of the Complete Psychological Works of Sigmund Freud. VI*. London: Hogarth.

Freud, S. (1908). On the sexual theories of children. *S.E., 9*.

Freud, S. (1913). Totem and taboo. *S.E., 13*.

Freud, S. (1917). On transformations of instinct as exemplified in anal erotism. *S.E., 17*.

Freud, S. (1922). Some neurotic mechanisms in jealousy, paranoia and homosexuality. *S.E.*, *18*.

Freud, S. (1939). Moses and monotheism. *S.E.*, *23*.

Freyd, J. J. (1996). *Betrayal Trauma*. Cambridge, MA: Harvard University Press.

Frith, C. (1994). "Theory of mind" in schizophrenia. In: A. S. David & J. C. Cutting (Eds.), *The Neuropsychology of Schizophrenia*. Hillsdale, NJ: Erlbaum.

Gabbard, G. (1996). *Psychodynamic Psychiatry in Clinical Practice*. Washington: American Psychiatric Press.

Gabbard, G. (2000). Disguise or consent. Problems and recommendations concerning the publication and presentation of clinical material. *International Journal of Psychoanalysis*, *81*: 1071–1086.

Gallup, J. (1982). *Feminism and Psychoanalysis. The Daughter's Seduction*. London: Macmillan.

Gedo, J. (1981). *Advances in Clinical Psychoanalysis*. New York: International Universities Press.

Gilbert, P. (1998). Evolutionary psychopathology. Why isn't the mind designed better than it is? *British Journal of Medical Psychology*, *71*: 353–373.

Gilbert, P., & McGuire, M. T. (1998). Shame, status and social roles: the psychobiological continuum from monkey to human. In: P. Gilbert & B. Andrews (Eds.), *Shame: Interpersonal Behaviour, Psychopathology and Culture*. New York: Oxford University Press.

Gilbert, P., & Bailey, K. G. (2000). *Genes on the Couch. Explorations in Evolutionary Psychotherapy*. Hove: Brunner-Routledge.

Gilbert, P., Bailey, K. G., & McGuire, M. T. (2000). Evolutionary psychotherapy. Principles and outline. In: P. Gilbert & K. G. Bailey (Eds.), *Genes on the Couch*. Hove: Brunner-Routledge.

Glantz, K., & Moehl, M.-B. (2000). Reluctant males. In: P. Gilbert & K. G. Bailey (Eds.), *Genes on the Couch*. Hove: Brunner-Routledge.

Green, A. (1982). Moral narcissism. *International Journal of Psychoanalytic Psychotherapy*, *7*: 243–269.

Green, B. (1979). The effect of distortions of the self. A study of the Picture of Dorian Gray. *Annual of Psychoanalysis*, *7*: 399–410.

Greenwald, D. F., & Harder, D. W. (1998). Domains of shame. Evolutionary, cultural, and psychotherapeutic aspects. In: P. Gilbert & B. Andrews (Eds.), *Shame, Interpersonal Behaviour, Psychopathology and Culture* New York: Oxford University Press.

Grotstein, J. S. (1977). The psychoanalytic concept of schizophrenia. II.

Reconciliation. *International Journal of Psycho-Analysis, 58*: 427–452.

Grotstein, J. S. (1990). The "black hole" as the basic psychotic experience: some newer psychoanalytic and neuroscience perspectives on psychosis. *Journal of the American Academy of Psychoanalysis, 18*: 29–46.

Grotstein, J. S. (2000). *Who is the Dreamer who Dreams the Dream? A Study of Psychic Presences*. Hillsdale, NJ: Analytic Press.

Grunberger, B. (1989). *New Essays on Narcissism*. London: Free Association Books.

Guntrip, H. (1968). *Schizoid Phenomena, Object Relations and the Self*. London: Hogarth.

Gurewich, J. F. (1999). Who's afraid of Jacques Lacan? In: J. F. Gurewich & M. Tort (Eds.), *Lacan and the New Wave in American Psychoanalysis. The Subject and the Self*. New York: Other Press.

Hamilton, W. D. (1964). The genetic evolution of social behavior. *Journal of Theoretical Biology, 7*: 1–52.

Harder, D. W. (1984). Character style of the defensively high self-esteem man. *Journal of Clinical Psychology, 40*: 26–35.

Harder, D. W. (1990). Comment on Wright et al. "Shame, guilt, narcissism, and depression: Correlates and sex differences." *Psychoanalytic Psychology, 7*: 285–289.

Hietanen, J. K., Surakka, V., & Linnankoski, I. (1998). Facial electromyographic responses to vocal affect expressions. *Psychophysiology, 35*: 530–536.

Jacobson, E. (1965). *The Self and the Object World*. London: Hogarth.

Joffe, W. G., & Sandler, J. (1967). Some conceptual problems involved in the consideration of disorders of narcissism. *Journal of Child Psychotherapy, 2*: 56–66.

Kahr, B. (2001). *Exhibitionism*. Cambridge: Icon Books.

Kalsched, D. (1996). *The Inner World of Trauma. Archetypal Defenses of the Personal Spirit*. London: Routledge.

Kernberg, O. (1975). *Borderline Conditions and Pathological Narcissism*. New York: Aronson.

Khan, M. (1972). *The Privacy of the Self*. London: Hogarth.

Kilborne, B. (1999). The disappearing who: Kierkegaard, shame and the self. In: J. Adamson & H. Clark (Eds.), *Scenes of Shame. Psychoanalysis, Shame and Writing*. Albany NY: State University of New York Press.

Klein, G. (1976). *Psychoanalytic Theory: An Exploration of Essentials*. New York: International Universities Press.

Klein, M. (1957). Envy and gratitude. In: *The Writings of Melanie Klein, Volume III*. London: Hogarth Press and the Institute of Psycho-Analysis, 1975.

Kohut, H. (1971). *The Analysis of the Self*. New York: International Universities Press.

Kohut, H. (1972). Thoughts on narcissism and narcissistic rage. *The Psychoanalytic Study of the Child*, 27: 360–400 [reprinted in (1978) *The Search for the Self: Selected Writings of Heinz Kohut, Volume 2*. New York: International Universities Press].

Kohut, H. (1977). *The Restoration of the Self*. New York: International Universities Press.

Kohut, H. (1984). *How Does Analysis Cure?* Chicago: University of Chicago Press.

Kohut, H. (1996). *The Chicago Institute Lectures*. P. Tolpin & M. Tolpin (Eds.). Hillsdale, NJ: The Analytic Press.

Lacan, J. (1977). *Ecrits*. London: Routledge.

Lewis, H. (1963). A case of watching as a defence against an oral incorporation fantasy. *Psychoanalytic Review*, 50(5): 68–80.

Lewis, H. (1971). *Shame and Guilt in Neurosis*. New York: International Universities Press.

Lewis, M. (1992). Self-conscious emotions and the development of self. In: T. Shapiro & R. N. Emde (Eds.), *Affect. Psychoanalytic Perspectives*. Maddison, Connecticut: International Universities Press.

Lichtenberg, J. (1983). *Psychoanalysis and Infant Research*. Hillsdale, NJ: Analytic Press.

Lichtenstein, H. (1961). Identity and sexuality. A study of their inter-relationship in man. *Journal of the American Psychoanalytic Association*, 9: 179–260.

Liotti, G. (2000). Disorganised attachment, models of borderline states and evolutionary psychotherapy. In: P. Gilbert & K. G. Bailey (Eds.), *Genes on the Couch*. London: Brunner-Routledge.

Lobsenz, N. M. (1975). Taming the green-eyed monster. In: G. Clanton & L. G. Smith (Eds.), *Jealousy*. Lanham, Maryland: University Press of America, 1998.

Lynd, H. (1958). *Shame and the Search for Identity*. New York: Science Edition.

Mead, G. H. (1934). *Mind, Self and Society*. Chicago: University of Chicago Press.

Mead, M. (1931). Jealousy: primitive and civilised. In: S. D. Schmalhausen & V. F. Calverton (Eds.), *Women's Coming of Age*. New York: Horace Liveright.

Meissner, W. W. (1986). *Psychotherapy and the Paranoid Process*. New York: Aronson.

Merleau-Ponty, M. (1964). *The Primacy of Perception*. Evanston, Ill: Northwestern University Press.

Migone, P., & Liotti, G. (1998). Psychoanalysis and cognitive-evolutionary psychology: an attempt at integration. *International Journal of Psychoanalysis, 79*: 1071–1095.

Mitchell, J. (1974). *Psychoanalysis and Feminism*. London: Allen Lane.

Mitchell, J. (2000). *Mad Men and Medusas. Reclaiming Hysteria and the Effects of Sibling Relations on the Human Condition*. London: Allen Lane.

Mollon, P. (1984). Shame in relation to narcissistic disturbance. *British Journal of Medical Psychology, 57*: 207–214.

Mollon, P. (1986). Narcissistic vulnerability and the fragile self. A failure of mirroring. *British Journal of Medical Psychology, 59*: 317–324.

Mollon, P. (1987). Self-awareness, self-consciousness, and preoccupation with self. In: K. Yardley & T. Honess (Eds.), *Self and Identity. Psychosocial Perspectives*. London: Wiley.

Mollon, P. (1993). *The Fragile Self. The Structure of Narcissistic Disturbance*. London: Whurr.

Mollon, P. (1996). *Multiple Selves. Multiple Voices. Working with Trauma, Violation and Dissociation*. Chichester: Wiley.

Mollon, P. (2001a). *Releasing the Self. The Healing Legacy of Heinz Kohut*. London: Whurr.

Mollon, P. (2001b). *The Unconscious*. Cambridge: Icon Books.

Mollon, P. (2002). *Remembering Trauma. A Psychotherapist's Guide to Memory and Illusion*. London: Whurr.

Mollon, P., & Parry, G. (1984). The fragile self. Narcissistic disturbance and the protective function of depression. *British Journal of Medical Psychology, 57*: 137–145.

Morrison, A. (1989a). *Shame. The Underside of Narcissism*. Hillsdale, NJ: The Analytic Press.

Morrison, A. (1989b). Shame and manic-depressive illness. In: *Shame. The Underside of Narcissism*. Hillsdale, NJ: The Analytic Press.

Nathanson, D. L. (1987a). A timetable for shame. In: D. L. Nathanson (Ed.), *The Many Faces of Shame*. New York: Guilford.

Nathanson, D. L. (1987b). Preface. In: D. L. Nathanson. (Ed.), *The Many Faces of Shame*. New York: Guilford.

Nathanson, D. L. (1992). *Shame and Pride. Affect, Sex and the Birth of the Self*. New York: Norton.

Neu, J. (1980). Jealous thoughts. In: A. O. Rorty (Ed.), *Explaining Emotions*. Berkeley: University of California Press.

Pao, P.-N. (1969). Pathological jealousy. *Psychoanalytic Quarterly, 38*: 616–638.

Piers, G., & Singer, A. (1953). *Shame and Guilt*. Springfield, Ill: Thomas.

Pines, M. (1995). The universality of shame. A psychoanalytic approach. *British Journal of Psychotherapy, 11*(3): 346–357.

Rado, S. (1928). The problem of melancholia. *International Journal of Psychoanalysis, 9*: 420–438.

Retzinger, S. M. (1998). Shame in the therapeutic relationship. In: P. Gilbert & B. Andrews (Eds.), *Shame: Interpersonal Behaviour, Psychopathology and Culture*. New York: Oxford University Press.

Riviere, J. (1932). Jealousy as a mechanism of defence. *International Journal of Psycho-Analysis, 13*: 414–424.

Rose, H., & Rose, S. (Eds.) (2000). *Alas Poor Darwin: Arguments Against Evolutionary Psychology*. London: Cape.

Rosenfeld, H. (1971). A clinical approach to the psychoanalytic theory of the life and death instincts: an investigation into the aggressive aspects of narcissism. *International Journal of Psycho-Analysis, 52*: 169–178 [reprinted in E. B. Spillius (Ed.), *Melanie Klein Today, Volume 1*. London: Routledge].

Rosenfeld, H. (1987). *Impasse and Interpretation: Therapeutic and Anti-therapeutic Factors in the Psychoanalytic Treatment of Psychotic, Borderline and Neurotic Patients*. London: Tavistock and The Institute of Psychoanalysis.

Sartre, J.-P. (1956). *Being and Nothingness. A Phenomenological Essay on Ontology*. New York: Philosophical Library Inc.

Schoenfeld, E. (1979). *Jealousy. Taming the Green Eyed Monster*. New York: Holt, Rinehart & Winston.

Schore, A. N. (1991). Early superego development. The emergence of shame and narcissistic affect regulation in the practicing period. *Psychoanalysis and Contemporary Thought, 14*: 187–250.

Schore, A. N. (1994). *Affect Regulation and the Origin of the Self*. Hillsdale, NJ: Erlbaum.

Schore, A. N. (1998). Early shame experiences and infant brain development. In: P. Gilbert & B. Andrews (Eds.), *Shame, Interpersonal Behaviour, Psychopathology and Culture*. New York: Oxford University Press.

Schore, A. N. (2000). Attachment and the regulation of the right brain. *Attachment and Human Development, 2*(1): 23–47.

Seidler, G. H. (2000). *In Others' Eyes. An Analysis of Shame*. Madison, Connecticut: International Universities Press.

Shengold, L. (1989). *Soul Murder. The Effects of Childhood Abuse and Deprivation*. New Haven: Yale University Press.

Slavin, J. H., & Pollock, L. (1997). The poisoning of desire: the destruction of agency and the recovery of psychic integrity in sexual abuse. *Contemporary Psychoanalysis, 33*(4): 573–593

Spielman, P. M. (1971). Envy and jealousy: an attempt at clarification. *The Psychoanalytic Quarterly, 40*: 59–82.

Spitz, R. (1965). *The First Year of Life*. New York: International Universities Press.

Steiner, J. (1993a). *Psychic Retreats: Pathological Organisations of the Personality in Psychotic, Neurotic and Borderline Patients*. London: Routledge.

Steiner, J. (1993b). Problems of psychoanalytic technique: patient-centered and analyst centered interpretations. In: *Psychic Retreats* (pp. 131–146). London: Routledge.

Steiner, J. (2000). Improvement, embarrassment and indignation. *Bulletin of the British Psychoanalytical Society, 36*(7): 2–9.

Steiner, J. (2002). The dread of exposure to humiliation and ridicule. West Lodge. Unpublished paper.

Stevens, A., & Price, J. (2000). *Evolutionary Psychiatry. A New Beginning. Second Edition*. London: Routledge.

Stoller, R. (1976). *Perversion. The Erotic Form of Hatred*. London: Harvester.

Symonds, D. (1979). *The Evolution of Human Sexuality*. New York: International Universities Press.

Tantam, D. (1991). Asperger syndrome in adulthood. In: U. Frith (Ed.), *Autism and Asperger Syndrome*. Cambridge: Cambridge University Press.

Thornhill, R., & Palmer, C. T. (2000). *A Natural History of Rape. Biological Bases of Sexual Coercion*. Cambridge, MA: MIT.

Thrane, G. (1979). Shame and the construction of the self. *Annual of Psychoanalysis, 7*: 321–341.

Torok, M. (1970). The significance of penis envy in women. In: J. Chasseguet-Smirgel (Ed.), *Female Sexuality. New Psychoanalytic Views* [reprinted by Maresfield/Karnac, London, 1985].

Tronick, E., Als, H., Adamson, L., Wise, S., & Brazelton, T. (1978). The infant's response to entrapment between contradictory messages in face-to-face interaction. *Journal of Child Psychiatry, 17*: 1–13.

Wenegrat, B. (1990). *Sociobiological Psychiatry*. Lexington, MA: Lexington Books.

White, G. L. (1980). Inducing jealousy: a power perspective. *Personality and Social Psychology Bulletin*, 6(2): 222–227.

White, G. L., & Mullen, P. E. (1989). *Jealousy: Theory, Research and Clinical Strategies*. New York: Guilford Press.

Wiederman, M. W., & Kendall, E. (1999). Evolution, sex and jealousy: investigation with a sample from Sweden. *Evolution and Human Behavior*, 20: 121–128.

Wilson, M., & Daly, M. (1992). The man who mistook his wife for a chattel. In: J. H. Barkow, L. Cosmides & J. Tooby (Eds.), *The Adapted Mind: Evolutionary Psychology and the Generation of Culture*. New York: International Universities Press.

Winnicott, D. W. (1960). Ego distortion in terms of true and false self. In: *The Maturational Processes and the Facilitating Environment*. London: Hogarth, 1979.

Winnicott, D. W. (1967). Mirror role of mother and family in child development. In: *Playing and Reality*. Harmondsworth: Penguin.

Wisdom, J. O. (1976). Jealousy in a twelve-month old boy. *International Review of Psycho-Analysis*, 3: 365–368.

Wright, K. (1991). *Vision and Separation between Mother and Infant*. London: Free Association.

Wurmser, L. (1999). "Man of the most dangerous curiosity": Nietzsche's "Fruitful and frightful vision" and his war against shame. In: J. Adamson & H. Clark (Eds.), *Scenes of Shame. Psychoanalysis, Shame and Writing*. Albany, NY: State University of New York Press.

INDEX